Global Justice

ONE WEEK LOAN

KEY CONCEPTS

Published

Barbara Adam, *Time*
Alan Aldridge, *Consumption*
Alan Aldridge, *The Market*
Colin Barnes and Geof Mercer, *Disability*
Darin Barney, *The Network Society*
Mildred Blaxter, *Health*
Harry Brighouse, *Justice*
Steve Bruce, *Fundamentalism*
Margaret Canovan, *The People*
Anthony Elliott, *Concepts of the Self*
Steve Fenton, *Ethnicity*
Michael Freeman, *Human Rights*
Russell Hardin, *Trust*
Fred Inglis, *Culture*
Jennifer Jackson Preece, Minority Rights
Paul Kelly, *Liberalism*
Anne Mette Kjær, *Governance*
Ruth Lister, *Poverty*
Jon Madel, *Global Justice*
Michael Saward, *Democracy*
John Scott, *Power*
Anthony D. Smith, *Nationalism*

Global Justice

Jon Mandle

polity

The right of Jon Mandle to be identified as Author of this Work has
been asserted in accordance with the UK Copyright, Designs and
Patents Act 1988.

First published in 2006 by Polity Press

Polity Press
65 Bridge Street
Cambridge CB2 1UR, UK

Polity Press
350 Main Street
Malden, MA 02148, USA

ISBN-10: 0-7456-3065-0
ISBN-13: 978-07456-3065-6
ISBN-10: 0-7456-3066-9 (pb)
ISBN-13: 978-07456-3066-3

A catalogue record for this book is available from the British Library.

Typeset in 10.5 on 12 pt Sabon
by Servis Filmsetting Ltd, Manchester
Printed and bound in Great Britain by TJ International Ltd, Padstow,
Cornwall

The publisher has used its best endeavours to ensure that the URLs for
external websites referred to in this book are correct and active at the
time of going to press. However, the publisher has no responsibility for
the websites and can make no guarantee that a site will remain live or
that the content is or will remain appropriate.

Every effort has been made to trace all copyright holders, but if any
have been inadvertently overlooked the publishers will be pleased to
include any necessary credits in any subsequent reprint or edition.

For further information on Polity, visit our website: www.polity.co.uk

for Anna

Contents

Preface   ix

1   Ethical Theory   1

2   Justice   15

3   Realism, Nationalism, and Cosmopolitanism   28

4   Human Rights   44

5   Challenges to Human Rights   59

6   Political Legitimacy   78

7   Poverty and Development   102

8   Globalization   125

Notes   152
References   160
Index   176

Preface

I began working on this project soon after completing a book on John Rawls's theory of justice (J. Mandle 2000b). I had written very little about Rawls's work on global justice, in part because I felt I didn't understand it well. To the extent that I had a view on the subject, I shared the perspective of those that I call "strong cosmopolitans." I was unable to see how Rawls could defend principles of global justice that are in crucial respects less demanding than his principles of domestic justice. Specifically, while I agreed that principles of *morality* must properly take into account special relationships among individuals, such as shared nationality, when it came to principles of *justice*, I could not identify a basis on which to distinguish sharply between domestic and global principles. A conversation with Josh Cohen put me on to what I now believe to be the right track. At about the same time, two articles were published (Wenar 2002; Blake 2001), and I read a third, unpublished piece (Bernstein, unpublished) that all pointed in the direction of a similar interpretation. As I proceeded to develop this line of thought, to my surprise – but not, it must be said, to the surprise of my friends and colleagues – my position moved closer and closer to how I now interpret Rawls (J. Mandle 2005). Although I believe that the position I defend is in broad agreement with Rawls's approach, in some important ways I depart from his method of presenting and defending his principles. For example, I do not invoke a hypothetical choice from an "original position."

The account of global justice that I develop here holds that there are basic human rights that are universal in two senses. First, every human being is entitled to enjoy these basic rights. Second, everyone has a duty of justice to respect these rights. That is, human rights generate duties that apply universally, although these duties may be of different strengths with respect to different people. My focus is on how these rights and duties are mediated through social institutions, including but not limited to political and legal institutions. Specifically, the protection of basic human rights requires the creation and maintenance of legitimate political institutions. When these institutions exist, they generate a distinction between fellow citizens and foreigners that is of direct importance to justice. Thus, while containing important cosmopolitan elements – the universality of human rights and the duties of justice that they generate – this account departs from the views of strong cosmopolitans by recognizing that justice makes fundamentally different demands on us concerning foreigners than it does concerning those with whom we share legitimate political institutions.

In some ways, this account cuts against the grain of a recent trend that de-emphasizes the importance and capacity of states in the face of pressures of globalization. It is certainly true that states are not the only actors in the world, and that when they do act, it is often under conditions not of their own choosing. Nonetheless, the world today and for the foreseeable future is one in which individuals and corporate actors pursue their goals against a background of rules and institutions created by states. This is not to say that states do or should enjoy a classical model of sovereignty, in which they pursue their narrow self-interest, unconstrained by morality or the interests of others. Rather, it is simply to point out that coercive, positive law is the creation of states and of the institutions to which they delegate that authority for specific purposes. It may not always have been that way, and it is possible to imagine alternatives; but in our world, states are the locus of coercive positive law, and this makes them unique from the point of view of justice. The account of global justice that I develop attempts to take proper account of the crucial relationship between states and legitimate law, while at the same time recognizing the importance of basic human rights and the cosmopolitan duties of justice that they generate.

Thanks go to the many people who helped in various ways, including Alyssa Bernstein, Chris Bertram, Michael Blake, Harry Brighouse, Josh Cohen, Jay Mandle, Joan Mandle, Darrel Moellendorf, Kai Nielsen, Thomas Pogge, David Reidy, Karen Schupack, Michel Seymour, Kok-Chor Tan, two anonymous referees, and audiences at the University at Albany, at the 2004 Pacific APA, and at the 2003 conference in Montreal honoring Kai Nielsen. Finally, at Polity, Louise Knight and Ellen McKinlay have been consistently patient and supportive, while offering valuable advice, and Jean van Altena did a superb job as copy-editor.

1
Ethical Theory

After many years of neglect, Anglo-American philosophers have begun to turn their attention to issues of global justice. Discussions of domestic justice flourished following the publication of *A Theory of Justice* by John Rawls in 1971 (Rawls 1999a). Until the 1990s, however, these discussions usually put aside questions of how a just society should relate to other societies and to non-citizens. There was a small philosophical literature on just war theory and scattered discussions of issues such as famine relief, but it is only recently that accounts of global justice have reached a critical mass, where many competing positions can productively engage one another. One important explanation of this recent flourishing is the collapse of Soviet communism. The Cold War was such a pervasive and overwhelming fact that for Anglo-American political theorists, at least, it tended to crowd out other topics in international relations. The dominant approach among policy analysts in the United States was a doctrine called "realism," which essentially holds that moral considerations do not apply to international relations (see chapter 3). I don't believe that most political philosophers agreed with this doctrine, but few explicitly challenged it. (Important exceptions included M. Cohen 1984; Beitz 1999, first published in 1979; and Shue 1996, first published in 1980.) With the collapse of Soviet communism, however, philosophers began to formulate more nuanced and less polarized principles to guide conduct toward foreign countries and people. There were suddenly many new options and attitudes to consider and to sort out.

A second explanation for the increased interest in global justice relates to the process of globalization. In the last three decades this process has brought more people and societies throughout the world into closer contact with one another than ever before. We will consider some aspects of globalization in chapter 8, but for now it is enough to note that this process has made the borders between countries seem less significant for many purposes. When Rawls wrote in 1971 that he would discuss "the justice of the law of nations and of relations between states" only "in passing" (Rawls 1999a: 7; cf. 331–3), it may not have seemed like a very significant omission. Three decades later, it is much more contentious. Cultural products and practices flow easily over borders; the economies of many countries depend heavily on foreign trade and investment; international organizations such as the United Nations and NATO authorize military action; and there has been a rapid proliferation of international non-governmental organizations addressing innumerable issues of concern and interest to people throughout the world. These developments have changed the issues and questions that political theorists confront as surely as did the collapse of the Soviet Union. New problems and possibilities have made some of their previous questions, approaches, and assumptions seem outdated. At least in part, it was being confronted with new circumstances and possibilities that led to the very rapid growth in the philosophical literature on global justice.

There is a general lesson here concerning the role of philosophy. The questions that philosophers ask, and the arguments with which they attempt to answer them, are often profoundly influenced by their social circumstances and the concrete issues and problems that their societies face. Yet, at the same time, the issues that political philosophers address tend to be subject to deep and persistent disagreement. As a result, philosophers must often rely on abstract concepts that may seem far removed from the concrete issues that often lie in the background of their work. We are often driven to these abstract concepts as a way to clarify our disagreements and uncertainties concerning more concrete and ordinary matters

(Rawls 1996: 44–6; J. Cohen 1986). If we are to resolve disagreements and uncertainties by giving reasons and making arguments, as philosophers aspire to do, we must proceed from shared assumptions about which we are confident. Abstract concepts often provide this common ground.

These abstract concepts must ultimately prove their worth by shedding light on the more concrete disagreements and uncertainties. Thus, it is appropriate and important that we test abstract concepts and claims against more concrete cases. If we are confident that slavery is a grave injustice, then any theory of justice had better identify slavery as unjust. If not, then we have a good reason to reject the proposed theory, whatever other virtues it might have. Although we may develop abstract concepts and theories to help resolve conflicts and uncertainties of a more concrete nature, these abstract concepts do not necessarily enjoy any kind of foundational priority over more particular judgments. We properly argue from whatever premises we are most confident about, at whatever level of generality or specificity, and attempt to generate arguments that establish conclusions where we are less confident or in disagreement (Rawls 2001: 29–32; J. Mandle 2000b: 45–55).

Consider, for example, a particular event: the military action taken by NATO in 1999 in response to the Serbian policy of "ethnic cleansing" in Kosovo. The background to this conflict is extremely complicated (see Judah 2002; Malcolm 1998), but here is a very brief summary. In the late 1990s, Kosovo was legally a province of Serbia with a population of approximately 2 million, almost 90 percent of whom were ethnic Albanians. By the fall of 1998, Serbs had driven some 250,000 ethnic Albanians from their homes. When the negotiations held in Rambouillet, France, failed, NATO commenced its threatened bombing of Serbia. The immediate result of the bombing was "a humanitarian catastrophe of incredible proportions . . . The Serbian forces moved quickly but systematically to eradicate the Albanian presence from Kosovo" (Luban 2002: 80). "In the end almost 850,000 were either deported or fled Kosovo and hundreds of thousands more were displaced inside" (Judah 2002: 241). "Before NATO intervened on March 24, approximately 2,500 people had died in Kosovo's civil war . . . During the 11 weeks of bombardment, an estimated 10,000 people died violently in the province, most of them Albanian civilians murdered by Serbs" (Mandelbaum 1999: 2–3). NATO stressed its own efforts to minimize civilian casualties, and although it did not release official estimates, in September 1999 General Joseph Galston, Vice-Chairman of the US Joint Chiefs of Staff, commented: "Despite the weight of bombs dropped, Serbian civilian casualties were amazingly light, estimated at less than 1,500 dead" (Amnesty International 2000: 33). After 77 days of bombing, Serbia agreed to remove all of its troops from Kosovo. By the end of 1999, the majority of Albanian refugees had returned home, and Kosovo is now administered by the UN as a protectorate.

Although these general facts are not in serious dispute, reasonable people disagree about whether the NATO campaign was justified. The point that I want to stress is that when we reflect on this question, we are immediately forced to consider more abstract issues. For some critics, the military campaign violated a simple and compelling moral principle: " 'First, do no harm.' If you can think of no way to adhere to that elementary principle, then do nothing; at least that is preferable to causing harm – the consequence recognized in advance to be 'predictable' in the case of Kosovo, a prediction amply fulfilled" (Chomsky 1999: 156). But is this Hippocratic principle itself defensible? Is it *never* morally permissible to do harm with the intention of preventing even greater harm? And if it is sometimes permissible, how should we decide whether killing "less than 1,500" civilians was a morally permissible price to pay? Consider further the fact that it is widely acknowledged that NATO's actions were contrary to existing international law, since they were not authorized by the UN Security Council. (The USA and its allies avoided bringing a resolution authorizing the use of force to the Security Council because they knew it would be subject to a veto by Russia.) How much weight should we give to existing international law? Finally, consider the fact that as NATO's Secretary-General Javier Solana observed, this was the first time that "a defensive alliance launched a military campaign to avoid a humanitarian tragedy outside its own borders" (Solana 1999: 114). For some critics, this humanitarian motive was exactly the problem. Realists, as we shall see, argue that countries should be concerned with their own national interest alone. In short, when we reflect on whether this particular military act was justified, we are drawn into more abstract disputes about moral principles, the significance of international law, and the proper goals of countries when dealing with other societies.

Like the assessment of the NATO campaign in Kosovo, the questions that we will be concerned with in this book are primarily *normative* in character. Normative questions involve asking for an *evaluation* of conduct, character, policy, or institutions. Because moral investigations are normative, they do not aim merely to describe the actual behavior of individuals or the design of existing institutions. Rather, they open up the possibility of criticism and of guiding conduct or designing institutions in new ways. Although I have stressed the social context in which philosophers do their work, contrary to Hegel's famous preface, the fact that social circumstances influence philosophical investigations does not mean that philosophy can only come on the scene too late to issue "instructions on how the world ought to be" (Hegel [1821] 1991: 23). Philosophy need not simply reflect and ratify changes that have already occurred. Instead, at its best, it can critically engage with the world, providing reflective insight into how things are, as well as guidance and hope concerning how they might be.

Ultimately, we are interested in normative questions, because we want to act properly. NATO faced a *choice* whether to pursue its campaign in Kosovo. We want to know whether the principles that guided its decisions were defensible, and whether they should be used to guide future conduct. The moral principles we develop, in other words, should be *action-guiding*. They should provide what philosophers call *practical reasons* – reasons why one should act or refrain from acting in one way or another. While it is in the nature of normative claims that they do not merely describe existing circumstances and practices, there is also a danger that they may become completely disconnected from their conditions of applicability. When this happens, normative claims are no longer useful guides – even indirect guides – and they become *utopian* in a pejorative sense. For example, we might assert that NATO was right to use military force against the Serbs, but that this should have been done in a way that did not result in any civilian casualties. Unfortunately, it is simply wishful thinking to believe that a military campaign can avoid all civilian casualties, and there is good reason to take the NATO commanders at their word that they attempted to minimize them. A theory that simply wishes away all unpleasant conditions can offer little practical guidance and may actually be dangerous. When we combine a critical, normative perspective with a realistic concern for what is possible, we will be led to construct what Rawls calls a "realistic utopia" (Rawls 1999b: 6, 11–12, 126–8), an idea to which we will return at the end of chapter 8.

There may seem to be something hopelessly misguided about trying to make the world a better place by generating yet more abstract philosophical arguments. After all, it might be said, morality is more about having the proper emotions and sympathetic identifications than about understanding abstract arguments. Richard Rorty, for example, makes such an objection when he argues that philosophical arguments cannot have much effect on people's behavior. He writes: "the most philosophy can hope to do is to summarize our culturally influenced intuitions about the right thing to do in various situations" (Rorty 1998: 171). Such summarizing is ineffective in actually convincing immoral people to become moral, he argues, since immoral people don't share the same underlying intuitions. Rather than generating philosophical arguments, we should "concentrate our energies on manipulating sentiments" (Rorty 1998: 176). Rorty is surely right that philosophy is not very effective at such manipulation – certainly not compared to novels, say, and other works of art.

However, Rorty assumes that we already know what morality requires, and that the only remaining question concerns how to manipulate others into behaving in the way that we know to be correct. His examples typically concern attitudes and actions that we can easily identify as evil – Serbs toward Muslims in the early 1990s, whites toward blacks under slavery, Nazis toward Jews in 1930s Germany. However, contrary to Rorty's suggestion, most philosophers don't assume that waving a philosophical argument will magically convince immoral people to become moral. The types of examples that Rorty cites certainly are important cases, in which we are confident that basic principles of justice are being violated in the grossest and most blatant ways possible.

We have no difficulty condemning in these cases precisely because we are so confident about the wrongs being done. But our condemnation of the Serbian policies and our sympathetic attunement to the plight of ethnic Albanians by themselves cannot determine whether NATO's bombing campaign was justified. Reasonable people with equally strong feelings of sympathetic identification may disagree with one another over whether the campaign was justified. Indeed, we ourselves may be unsure, reluctant to declare the reasons on either side superior to those on the other. When we face such dilemmas, it is of little help to be told to "consult our sentiments" or to "follow our heart." What we need to do is to consider the strength and nature of the reasons on each side, in order to help us make up our minds.

Questions about morality are often met with the rhetorical question, "But who's to say?" This question is often intended to shut down further discussion and reflection. If made explicit, the skeptical thought expressed by this question might be something like this: what a person has reason to do is strongly dependent on his or her particular situation, and no other person is ever in as good a position to make that judgment as the agent herself – each individual is her own judge alone. Such a position can serve as a useful reminder of the dangers of becoming a "moralizer." A moralizer is someone who makes moral judgments without a subtle or nuanced appreciation of the detailed specifics of an actual case. In many circumstances, it is perfectly possible and appropriate to withhold judgment, at least until one becomes better informed. But sometimes we are confident that we have adequate knowledge of the particular case, or the circumstances demand that we make a determination one way or the other – should NATO bomb or not? Taken literally, the answer to the question "Who's to say?" is that we are *all* to say, as best we can, considering as much of the relevant information as possible. There is nothing in principle that excludes anyone from making their best judgment after reflecting on the applicable normative principles and relevant features of the particular case. On the other hand, a modesty born of suspicion of moralizers remains appropriate.

Often, there is an implicit assumption of relativism hiding behind the "Who's to say?" question. There are various forms of relativism that are not often distinguished from one another, but the form that we will consider here says that the only moral standards against which to assess an action or institution are the principles accepted by the members of the particular society in which the action is performed or the institution is located. The relativist says that while it makes sense to evaluate individual conduct and institutions by the standards of the particular society in which they are located, it is inappropriate or impossible to evaluate the standards themselves. The way of life of a society is foundational, in the sense that there is no external perspective from which to evaluate it.

Let us call a person who denies relativism in this sense a "universalist." It is important to note that a universalist, as defined here, need only say that it is *sometimes* possible and appropriate to make a moral assessment not based on the standards or practices affirmed in the local society. In other words, a universalist can still agree that *some*, perhaps even *most*, evaluations depend on local context and practice. The universalist need not be a moralizer and may be modest in making moral assessments. The question is whether it is *ever* appropriate to make moral assessments that would not be widely accepted in the society in question. It is appropriate to consider this extreme version of relativism here, because only it represents a fundamental challenge to our project.[1]

Defenders of relativism almost always stake their case on "the impressiveness of the variation in ethical belief to be found across human history and culture" (Wong 1991: 443). The earliest example in Western philosophy of such an argument was written by the Greek historian Herodotus in 440 BCE. Herodotus reports that Darius, the king of Persia (what is now Iran), was impressed with the diversity of practices in different societies and set up an experiment to test this diversity.

> [He] summoned the Greeks who happened to be present at his court, and asked them what they would take to eat the dead bodies of their fathers. They replied that they would not do it for any money in the world. Later, in the presence of the Greeks, and through an interpreter, so [that] they could understand what was said, he asked some Indians, of the tribe called Callatiae, who do in fact eat their parents' dead bodies, what they would take to burn them. They uttered a cry of horror and forbade him to mention such a dreadful thing. (Herodotus [440 BCE] 1954: 219–20)

Herodotus concludes that this anecdote confirms the saying that custom is "king of all" – that is, that in justifying one's behavior, there is no higher court of appeal than the practices that prevail in one's own society. In the sixteenth century, Michel de Montaigne stated the position very clearly: "every man calls barbarous anything he is not accustomed to; it is indeed the case that we have no other criterion of truth or right-reason than the example and form of the opinions and customs of our own country" (Montaigne [1580] 1987: 231).

Relativism does not follow as immediately from the fact of diversity as Herodotus seemed to think. As David Wong, himself a defender of a moderate form of relativism, writes, "The simple fact of diversity in belief is no disproof of the possibility that there are some beliefs better to have than the others because they are truer or more justified than the rest" (Wong 1991: 444). But defenders of relativism have three further arguments. First, they sometimes say that the meaning of moral terms is relative to a particular society or linguistic group. Second, they say that moral disagreements are persistent in a way that scientific disagreements are not. Third, they say that relativism is necessary to provide a basis for recognition of diverse values and toleration. I don't believe that these arguments succeed, but it is important to see why not.

The first argument, based on a claim about linguistic meaning, is a non-starter. Occasionally an author will assert something like the following: "morality differs in every society, and is a convenient term for socially approved habits. Mankind has always preferred to say, 'It is morally good,' rather than 'It is habitual,' and the fact of this preference is matter enough for a critical science of ethics. But historically the two phrases are synonymous" (Benedict 2001: 87; cf. Sumner 2001: 76). As a claim about the meaning of terms, this is simply false. It is possible to criticize the practices of a society without contradicting oneself or using moral vocabulary incorrectly. As Will Kymlicka forcefully points out, "When a Muslim woman in Egypt says 'Sexual discrimination is wrong,' she does *not* mean 'We don't do that around here.' On the contrary, she is saying this precisely because it *is* done around there and may indeed be very firmly embedded in all the myths, symbols, and institutions of her history and society. She might also say 'Discrimination is wrong (although it is approved around here)' " (Kymlicka 1989: 66). If the meaning of "moral" were identical to "habitual for a community," then the Muslim woman would be contradicting herself when she attempts to express her criticism. But it seems clear that we can use moral language to evaluate not only individuals and actions, but societies and practices even when they are widely accepted.

The second argument for relativism claims that moral disagreements are persistent, even intractable, in a way that scientific controversies are not. This shows, defenders claim, that there is no "fact of the matter" about what morality demands that is independent of the different attitudes of various societies and their practices. There are several replies to this argument. One reply attempts to explain the persistence of moral disagreement by finding sources of error in our moral judgments that are not typically present in scientific investigations. For example, it is sometimes claimed that our investigation into moral issues is more subject to influence and distortion by our own particular interests than are scientific investigations. Thomas Nagel observes that when "strong interests are involved which will be affected by different answers to a disputed question" we should "expect extreme variation of belief and radical disagreement." Such interests are "present throughout ethics to a uniquely high degree" (Nagel 1986: 148). People have very strong psychological tendencies to see themselves as acting morally. This leads to many forms of rationalization (in the pejorative sense) and to the phenomenon of "walling off," in which people fail to connect beliefs that would jointly entail a conclusion that they would prefer not to face. Judith Jarvis Thomson, who describes this phenomenon in detail, gives the example of George Washington, who, when asked about his views on slavery, replied, "I shall frankly declare to you that I do not like even to think, much less talk, of it" (Harman and Thomson, 1996: 205). So this reply concedes that practical disagreements are more persistent than scientific disagreements, but it tries to provide an explanation of this that does not lead to relativism.

A second strategy for the universalist is to deny that moral diversity is as deep as the relativist suggests. Many apparently different moral evaluations may hide deeper agreement. For example, while the Greeks and the Indians whom Herodotus described were morally appalled by the others' treatment of the dead, this may have concealed deeper agreement. For example, each may have believed that it is morally required to show proper respect for the dead. The disagreement concerned which practice expressed the appropriate respect. A universalist can say that what morality requires is respect, but that respect can be expressed in different ways according to various conventional practices – no ceremony is intrinsically better than another. If moral principles are expressed in highly abstract language, it appears that there are principles that are (at least nearly) universal to all societies. As George Silberbauer observes: "it seems that sociability is a universal human trait and reciprocity appears to be a functional necessity of sustained relationships. Respect for human life could perhaps also be regarded as a universal value, but is subject to wide variation in the extent of recognition and of priority accorded to life preservation relative to other interests" (Silberbauer 1991: 27; cf. Moody-Adams 1997). The flip side of this strategy would be to argue that in the population as a whole, disagreements concerning scientific matters are far more persistent than is commonly assumed. For example, evolutionary theory may form the core of modern biology, but a recent opinion poll found that only one-third of Americans believe it to be well supported by evidence, and 45 percent believe that "God created human beings pretty much in their present form about 10,000 years ago" (Newport 2004). It is only when we focus on a narrow group of specialists that a consensus emerges. With a comparably selective focus, we could also generate substantial ethical agreement.

The third argument that is sometimes made for relativism, and the one that I believe is typically at the core of the relativist impulse, holds that only relativism can underwrite the idea of respect for diversity. As we have seen, however, a universalist can agree that some moral matters – such as which ceremony best expresses respect – depend on local practices and attitudes. Furthermore, relativism provides an extremely flimsy basis for supporting the worthy impulse toward toleration. After all, to say that a society should tolerate the practices or ways of life of another society is itself to make a normative claim. Relativism says that such normative claims can be justified only on the basis of the existing practices of a particular society. This means that, according to relativism, if a society has a traditional practice of toleration toward others, then it is proper for that society to tolerate others. On the other hand, if a society has a tradition of intolerance toward others, the proper attitude for that society would be one of intolerance, and a tolerant attitude would actually be wrong. Consider the following events, as related by Jared Diamond (1997: 53–4), that took place in 1835 in the Chatham Islands, 500 miles east of New Zealand. The Moriori people "were a small isolated population of hunter-gatherers, equipped with only the simplest technology and weapons, entirely inexperienced at war, and lacking strong leadership or organization." The Maori, in contrast, living in New Zealand, were from a "dense population of farmers chronically engaged in ferocious wars, equipped with more-advanced technology and weapons, and operating under strong leadership." Two ships carrying a total of 900 Maori soldiers armed with guns, clubs, and axes arrived on the islands. The invaders announced that they were enslaving the Moriori and proceeded to kill those who resisted. "An organized resistance by the Moriori could still then have defeated the Maori, who were outnumbered two to one. However, the Moriori had a tradition of resolving disputes peacefully." They chose not to fight back. Over the course of several days, the Maori "killed hundreds of Moriori, cooked and ate many of the bodies, and enslaved all the others, killing most of them too over the next few years as it suited their whim." A Maori conqueror explained: "We took possession . . . in accordance with our customs and we caught all the people. Not one escaped. Some ran away from us, these we killed, and others we killed – but what of that? It was in accordance with our custom." Assuming these actions were, in fact, in accordance with Maori custom, this defense of genocide is unanswerable within the framework of relativism.

There are additional problems with relativism that are worth briefly pointing out. As can be seen implicitly in the previous criticism, relativism underwrites an extreme and unwarranted conservative attitude. In effect, it says that unless a principle or practice is currently endorsed by a society, there is no basis for defending it. This holds for *internal* dissenters as well as external critics. Imagine a Maori warrior questioning the rampage of his fellows, arguing that the Moriori are peaceful, that they have done the Maori no wrong, that they have a right to live as they see fit, etc. Relativism would rule out such a challenge. Similarly, according to the relativist, there could be no moral arguments available to Abolitionists in the southern United States in the mid-nineteenth century or to civil rights reformers in the mid-twentieth century. The point is not simply that such reformers are fighting against heavy odds or that it will be difficult for them to convince the majority to change their attitudes. Rather, the relativist is making a substantive judgment that their causes are *wrong* because the claims of the reformers conflict with the practices and attitudes of their societies. This is an untenable position. It is at least possible to believe that reformers – even radical reformers – may be correct even when they resist well-established practices.

Yet another problem for relativism stems from the fact that virtually all societies are characterized by some degree of internal diversity. This includes not only modern, pluralistic states, but also the "exotic" societies studied by the pioneering anthropologists (Moody-Adams 1997: esp. ch. 1). Relativists face a problem when they appeal to traditions and practices that are themselves subject to conflicting interpretations. Which interpretation should the relativist rely on? It is often a matter of internal dispute how an accepted practice should be extended in new circumstances. The relativist can offer no guidance in such circumstances, yet these are arguably the conditions in which help is most needed. The final problem for relativism is perhaps the most obvious, given the concerns of this book. Some institutions and practices involve cooperation among agents from different societies and traditions. What principles would relativism say we should use when assessing such institutions? When relativism says that each social unit should follow its own traditions and practices, this assumes that we can identify a single tradition or practice that is authoritative within each of these units. In an era of increasing international institutions and internal diversity within societies, however, this assumption is false.

Despite all of these criticisms, relativism does get something right, and it is important to see what that is. When the field of anthropology was being developed in the nineteenth century, it was premised on a hierarchy of societies. "Influenced by

Darwinian theory, early anthropological theory tended to arrange the peoples and social institutions of the world in an evolutionary series, from primordial man to the civilized human beings of nineteenth-century Europe" (Wong 1991: 447). This theory lent support to the imperialism of European states. But in the mid-twentieth century, many anthropologists "came to see the peoples they studied as intelligent men and women whose lives had meaning and integrity. And this led to questioning the basis for implicit judgements of the inferiority of their ways of life, especially after the spectacle of the civilized nations in brutal struggle with one another in the First World War" (Wong 1991: 447). What often underlies relativism is an admirable rejection of racism and imperialism, together with a commitment to recognizing that valuable lives come in many different forms and can be found in many different circumstances. Detailed knowledge of specific practices and societies is necessary to make any kind of informed judgment about a society. Moralizing can often be ugly and ignorant. I have argued, however, that relativism does not provide an adequate framework within which one can defend principled toleration of diversity.

Few philosophers who defend relativism embrace the extreme form that we have been discussing. Most are more moderate, and would reject with horror the thought that their views could be used to defend a "Nazi morality" or the actions of the Maori. Instead, they say that "A more reasonable version of normative relativism would have to permit us to pass judgement on others with substantially different values" (Wong 1991: 448; cf. Wong 1984: 59–60). So, a more moderate relativism would say that we should be tolerant of different ways of life and social organizations, but that this toleration needs to be grounded in a framework that can be used to evaluate the permissibility of these different practices. What is needed, therefore, is an account of the principles to be used in making such normative judgments that does not succumb to crude moralizing.

2
Justice

We concluded chapter 1 by criticizing relativism, but also by emphasizing that the basic impulse behind relativism is frequently an admirable commitment to toleration. Some people may be tempted by relativism because they appreciate the wide diversity of ways of life in which people can flourish and live meaningful and valuable lives. Appearances to the contrary, however, relativism – at least in the extreme form we discussed – cannot support this appreciation. What we need are moral principles that recognize and respond appropriately to diversity. Liberal conceptions of justice, and John Rawls's idea of political liberalism in particular, attempt to do precisely this. In this chapter we will examine this approach to justice, focusing primarily on issues of domestic justice, before proceeding to consider whether and how this approach should be modified to address issues of global justice.

Modern liberalism began to take shape in European philosophy during the seventeenth and eighteenth centuries, largely in response to religious strife. After the Reformation, European societies were populated by members of rival religions, each of which asserted with the certainty of faith that it alone held the path to true salvation. It was not at all clear whether stable and tolerant political institutions were even possible in such circumstances. Rawls points out that "Intolerance was accepted as a condition of social order and stability" (Rawls 1996: p. xxvii). As a result, as one historian observes, "During the century and a half between 1559 and 1715, Europe was in a nearly constant state of war. There were fewer than thirty years of international peace, and more than a hundred years of major combat, in which all or most of the leading European states were simultaneously engaged" (Dunn 1979: 1). During the Thirty Years' War, which lasted from 1618 to 1648, for example, "The German cities lost one third of their population, and the rural areas two fifths of their population . . . The empire had seven or eight million fewer inhabitants in 1648 than in 1618" (Dunn 1979: 89). These catastrophic losses were due not only directly to fighting, but also indirectly to disease and famine brought on by peasant populations fleeing from advancing armies. It gradually emerged that if there were to be a peaceful resolution, it would come not from imposing on nonbelievers the one true faith, but rather through some form of toleration. Initially, this realization was accepted reluctantly as an unfortunate practical necessity. The Peace of Westphalia, which concluded the Thirty Years' War, is commonly taken to mark the birth of the modern international order of independent and sovereign states, although this may be more symbolic than historically accurate (Krasner 1999: esp. 77–81). The form of toleration adopted was very limited, since the Peace did not require states to practice internal toleration, but merely allowed each state to determine and impose its own religious affiliation on its population. More generally, it enshrined into international law the idea of non-interference in the domestic affairs of sovereign states. Although often violated (not least through colonization), it was only with the emergence of a doctrine of human rights in the mid-twentieth century that this strong notion of state sovereignty was seriously challenged in international law.

Gradually, toleration came to be viewed as more than an unfortunate compromise necessitated by the balance of power between rivals. The toleration of diversity came to have moral support of its own, and over time it expanded within societies, not only among them. As Rawls conjectures, "Perhaps the doctrine of free faith developed because it is difficult, if not impossible, to believe in the damnation of those with whom we have, with trust and confidence, long and fruitfully cooperated in maintaining a just society" (Rawls 1996: p. xxvii). To be sure, there were other important factors in the development of liberalism, such as the early successes of modern science and the emergence of centralized bureaucratic states, but the experience of devastating religious warfare was a crucial element.

Like European societies themselves, philosophers only gradually accommodated themselves to the new realities of diverse societies and their distinctive problems. From ancient times, ethical theories typically aimed to identify the nature of the good life for human beings, and much moral philosophy continues this project today. However, following the Reformation and the Wars of Religion, a different question pressed itself with great urgency: Is it possible to have a just and stable society in which people hold different views about the nature of the good life (including religious matters)? In addressing this question, the problem is not to identify which way of life, religious faith, highest good, or comprehensive ethical theory is correct. Rather, it is to find social principles that are fair to, and can be recognized to be fair by, people who disagree about these fundamental matters. In circumstances of deep and persistent disagreement about the nature of salvation, for example, societies organized around the aim of saving everyone's soul threaten to provoke the kind of fight to the death that characterized European societies during the seventeenth century. Rather than the achievement of a particular goal such as salvation or a specific conception of the good life, philosophers began to develop a new orientation: a good society would be one that aimed at the fair treatment of its citizens. This liberal approach, in other words, focused on the virtue of social justice.

There were, and are, critics of such liberal theories of justice. Michael Sandel, for example, argues that "in some cases, justice is not a virtue but a vice" (Sandel 1998: 34). Justice, Sandel believes, is "a remedial virtue, whose moral advantage consists in the repair it works on fallen conditions" (p. 32). In other words, according to Sandel, the need for justice may itself reflect a significant moral loss that even the achievement of perfect justice cannot rectify. Sandel views justice as regulating the interaction of individuals who think of themselves as isolated from and indifferent, if not hostile, to one another. Only because they are not moved by a deep identification with one another, must their interactions be artificially regulated by principles of justice. Wouldn't it be better if we cared for and identified with each other in the first place, thereby avoiding the conflicts that must be resolved by considerations of justice? Sandel concedes that justice is sometimes an important virtue, "but only conditionally, as physical courage is to a war zone" (p. 31).

I believe that Sandel is mistaken, but his criticism brings out an important point. Although social justice is not predicated on individuals being selfish, as Sandel sometimes suggests, it is a virtue designed to respond to the possibility of conflict and disagreement. Specifically, justice responds to the diversity of comprehensive ethical and religious doctrines and to the different values and goals that people find worth pursuing. As Stuart Hampshire puts it in a book entitled *Justice is Conflict*: "Within any nation there will always be contests arising not only from conflicting interests, particularly economic interest, but also from competing moral outlooks and entrenched beliefs" (Hampshire 2000: 79). Some goals conflict with one another directly, in that achieving one is logically incompatible with achieving another. If you and I each aim to become the fastest runner in the world, I cannot achieve my goal if you achieve yours. More typically, however, conceptions of the good conflict with one another only indirectly. If social resources are directed toward one person's goals, usually there will be fewer resources for another's. It is a permanent fact about the human condition that resources are limited, and this fact, together with the diversity of conceptions of the good life, generates the potential for conflict. A political theory based on the assumption that at some point we will be able to transcend such conflicts would be utopian in the pejorative sense.

Furthermore, these potential conflicts are not (only) the result of excessive selfishness. Adherents of rival religious faiths may fight to the death because they believe that God has ordered them to do so. Though they may not appreciate the value of diversity, and may be acting unethically and unreasonably, it would be inaccurate to call them selfish. They are not pursing narrow, self-interested gain. More generally, there can be conflicts among ways of life that are not in themselves immoral or unreasonable. Indeed, free societies must be expected to generate a wide diversity of ways of life, each of which, while reasonable, nonetheless conflicts with others. Uniformity can only be achieved, if at all, through brutal oppression. If one thinks of diversity and the resulting possibility of conflict as a fallen condition to be overcome, as Sandel does, one is simply regretting the existence of freedom itself.

To say that free societies will engender diverse and conflicting ways of life is not to say that these conflicts will always be realized through a fight to the death, or even through overt hostility. A liberal society aims to regulate and mediate these conflicts in a way that all can recognize as fair. In doing so, it takes social justice to be its primary virtue. Just as prudence is the virtue that responds to our all-too-common shortsightedness, and generosity is the virtue that responds to our tendency toward selfishness, so social justice is the virtue that responds to the possibility of conflict among reasonable values and ends. Political liberalism, in defending principles of social justice to regulate such conflicts, self-consciously avoids developing a complete account of the ethical life that would require determining which way of life or conception of the good life is best.

Over time, liberalism gradually developed and refined two elements. First, there are substantive principles of toleration, individual liberty, and equality. These include, for example, guarantees of civil and political rights for all citizens. The second element consists in what we might think of as a liberal method of justification. According to this approach, principles for the organization of society are to be defended and justified in terms that could be accepted by the people who are to live under them. The most vivid illustration of this approach to justification is found in the idea of a social contract. Although there are many different social contract arguments, what is common among them is that principles are to be justified through the agreement (explicit or tacit, actual or hypothetical) of citizens. Historically, the substantive and the methodological commitments of liberalism did not always develop together. Hobbes, for example, found little need for guarantees of freedom of speech, while nonetheless adhering strongly to the view that principles of political morality had to be justified in terms that each individual could accept. Bentham, by contrast, defended religious toleration on the grounds that he knew with scientific certainty the nature of the good toward which all action was directed: namely, pleasure. However,

I take these two elements together to be constitutive of modern liberalism and its approach to social justice. We will first focus on the method of justification, before briefly considering the content of the principles appropriate for assessing the justice of a society.

Rawls (1996) argues that when it comes to developing principles of basic social justice for a society, we should construct what he calls a "political conception of justice." This is a technical term and does not simply mean that the principles concern political matters. The basic idea is that the justification of the principles of justice should not depend on the truth of any particular comprehensive ethical theory, account of the good life, or religion (Rawls 1996: 11–15). Instead, we should be able to provide a justification that can be recognized and accepted by reasonable people who disagree about these fundamental matters.[1] But why, some might ask, wouldn't an argument based on our sincerely held (although controversial) religious or ethical beliefs be enough?[2] One possible answer, suggested by the historical origin of liberalism, is that if a diverse society organizes itself around principles acceptable only to members of a certain religion, it will inevitably break down into civil war. While there certainly is historical precedent for this, and while it may be the tendency in some societies, it certainly overstates the case as a general thesis. Not all unjust societies, let alone all societies based on a single comprehensive doctrine, inevitably degenerate into civil war.

To understand the ethical reason for developing a political conception of justice, we must consider more closely the object to be evaluated. A political conception of justice is designed for evaluating what Rawls calls "the basic structure of society": the system formed by the fundamental political, economic, and social institutions of a society. There are several reasons to make this the primary object of evaluation, but two are especially important for us. The first is simply that the basic structure has such a momentous impact on virtually all aspects of life. Not only does it influence decisively who gets what, but it fundamentally shapes our identities and self-conceptions. Few would deny that the political, economic, and social circumstances into which an individual is born will profoundly affect that individual's life prospects and is therefore of great ethical significance.

The second important point is that, in addition to having such a profound influence on all members of a society, the basic structure of society is coercively imposed on them. The fact is that if citizens are to live together in a single society, they have no choice but to share a single basic structure. By contrast, they do not have to share a single religion or agree about the nature of the good life. As noted above, it wasn't always apparent that a religiously tolerant society could remain stable, but history has shown this to be a real possibility. By contrast, it simply doesn't make sense to talk about a single society with more than one basic structure. Such an arrangement would not be a single society at all. Notice that in opting for religious toleration, as opposed to imposing a single faith on everyone, a society as a whole is making a collective decision. It is choosing to impose religious tolerance on those who might prefer their society to engage in persecution. Similarly, a society makes a single, collective decision when it decides to go to war, to recognize and enforce a certain kind of property right, to impose taxes, and to protect certain endangered species. The important point is that in making collective decisions of these kinds, a society imposes its decision on everyone, including on those who would believe the decisions to be misguided. In some cases, we think that justice requires imposing conformity, such as when a society prohibits people from assaulting one another. In other cases, we think it would be wildly unjust to impose conformity, say by requiring everyone to engage in the same religious practice. In between these extremes are the many cases in which a society may choose through its political institutions whether or not to impose a single decision upon itself. Notice that the design of the political structure is itself a collective choice that is part of the basic structure of society and is imposed on all. This choice is a kind of higher-order collective decision. It specifies a procedure according to which other collective decisions are to be made – for example, through the creation of law.

There is a crucial difference between holding a particular view to be correct – say, a view concerning the nature of God or the good life – and taking the truth of this view to justify the use of force against those who disagree. Consider a debate between two devout religious believers of different faiths concerning the proper form of worship. Each, we can imagine, marshals her best arguments and quotes her favorite passages from Scripture. It is possible, of course, that one will succeed in convincing the other to adopt her beliefs and practices. But suppose that neither succeeds in convincing the other, and each continues to believe that the other is profoundly mistaken. At this point, it is possible for one of them to try to force the other to change her practices and adopt what she takes to be the correct form of worship. However, in order to justify such a coercive act, she must say more than simply that the other is wrong. To justify coercion, she must say something like this: by engaging in a false form of worship, she is endangering her eternal soul; or, although she can't see it now, once she engages in the correct practice for a while, she will come to recognize its value; or, her form of worship is not only mistaken, it is destabilizing and dangerous to the social order. Whether any of these arguments is sufficient to justify her coercion is another matter, but the point is that the use of force against a person is never justified *simply* by showing that they are mistaken. There is a gap between saying that someone is doing something wrong and saying that they should be coerced into acting in the correct way. This is not simply a theoretical point, and it is worth pausing to consider an example.

Many different religions and comprehensive doctrines recognize the difference between being committed to a particular religious faith or way of life and coercively imposing on others institutions that can be justified only on the basis of it. The Catholic Church, to choose but a single example, embraces religious tolerance at the level of the state, despite being fully committed to the truth of certain religious dogmas and to the belief that anyone who rejects those dogmas is mistaken. In 1967, as a product of the Second Vatican Council, Pope Paul VI issued the Declaration on Religious Freedom *Dignitatis Humanae*, which reaffirmed the Church's traditional view that the "one true religion subsists in the Catholic and Apostolic Church, to which the Lord Jesus committed the duty of spreading it abroad among all men." But it also insisted that "the human person has a right to religious freedom. This freedom means that all men are to be immune from coercion on the part of individuals or of social groups and of any human power, in such wise that no one is to be forced to act in a

manner contrary to his own beliefs, whether privately or publicly, whether alone or in association with others within due
limits. . . . This right of the human person to religious freedom
is to be recognized in the constitutional law whereby society is
governed and thus it is to become a civil right." Furthermore,
since a human being is "endowed with reason and free will . . .
the right to religious freedom has its foundation . . . in his very
nature. . . . It follows that a wrong is done when government
imposes upon its people, by force or fear or other means, the
profession or repudiation of any religion, or when it hinders
men from joining or leaving a religious community" (Paul VI
1967). The Catholic Church is certainly not organized inter-
nally according to liberal principles. Yet, it is able to recognize
the distinction between holding a view to be true and coercively imposing it (or institutions that can only be based on it)
on nonbelievers.

While there is a gap between believing that a certain religious practice or way of life is best and coercively imposing it
on others, there is *no such gap* when it comes to the design of
the basic structure of society. An argument for a particular
constitutional arrangement, for example, simply *is* an argument for coercively imposing that structure on all members of
the society. Such an argument might not specify in detail how
the structure is to be created or maintained, and of course we
might reject an institution that would otherwise be attractive
if there is no realistic and morally acceptable path that could
bring it about. However, the crucial point, to repeat, is that the
basic structure of society is something that must be imposed
on all citizens, ultimately through the coercive apparatus
of the state, whether or not they individually agree with it.
Furthermore, the imposition of this object is of profound
importance to everyone's life prospects. In order to justify
such a coercive imposition on people, it is not enough to argue
that it would be good according to some particular comprehensive ethical theory, view of the good life, or religion.
Rather, because an argument for a certain basic structure is,
and must be, an argument for its coercive imposition, there is
a higher standard for such a justification. We must offer an
argument in terms that all reasonable people could accept,
regardless of other continued disagreements. We must, in
other words, develop a political conception of justice.

Before moving on, I want to pause to emphasize one crucial, yet often misunderstood point. For the reasons we have just been discussing, liberalism focuses on the virtue of social justice. But it does not deny that other virtues, such as fortitude, temperance, prudence, courage, generosity, modesty, and loyalty, may be important.[3] Each of these can be characterized by certain actions and attitudes that are appropriate in various circumstances, and most comprehensive ethical theories will provide an account of these and other virtues. Liberalism, with its emphasis on justice, tries to avoid entering into controversies about how these virtues are to be understood and how each is to be weighed against other considerations. This agnosticism about the further virtues, however, must not be confused with skepticism. To illustrate the difference, consider the difference between a state that grants wide religious liberty and does not enforce any particular religion and a state that takes atheism to be correct, requires government officials to deny the existence of God, and prohibits the practice of traditional religions. We could mark the difference between these two states by saying that the first is committed to agnosticism at the state level, while the second endorses atheism. A similar distinction holds at the methodological level. We must distinguish between an argument for principles of justice that does not rely on any particular religious truths, on the one hand, and one that assumes that all (traditional) religious beliefs are false, on the other. If we aim to provide justifications of principles of justice that are acceptable to people holding different religious beliefs, we obviously cannot rely on arguments that presuppose the truth of some particular religion. But equally, we can't rely on arguments that assume that all religious faiths are false. An argument based on atheism would obviously not be acceptable to those who hold a religious faith. Rather, our only prospect is to maintain agnosticism on religious questions and attempt to produce arguments that rely on other, non-religious premises. Exactly the same point holds more generally for comprehensive ethical and philosophical doctrines and conceptions of the good life, and a liberal society will attempt to justify its principles of justice without affirming or denying that any particular one is true.

So, a society that affirms a liberal conception of justice tolerates a wide range of religions, ways of life, and comprehensive ethical doctrines. It remains agnostic concerning the truth of these doctrines, but this agnosticism should not be confused with skepticism. Official agnosticism about these matters at the state level does not imply that individuals must give up their particular doctrines. On the contrary, individual citizens are typically not agnostic about these fundamental matters, although, of course, they may be. They are free to hold and to reflect upon their religious and ethical beliefs, and they may revise them, if they choose, although their beliefs need not be fully explicit or even coherent.

We are now in a position to consider briefly the content of the principles that a political conception of justice would generate for evaluating the basic structure of a single society. Because the principles underwrite institutions that will be coercively imposed on all individuals, we must do more than simply argue that they are acceptable according to a particular religion or comprehensive ethical theory. We must argue that, regardless of the particular religion or comprehensive ethical doctrine that they hold, all reasonable people could accept them. Since the principles are to be justified to all reasonable individuals equally, it is no surprise that they involve some kind of equal treatment. If the principles were to treat anyone unfairly, he or she would in effect veto them. One of the persistent controversies in such theories, however, concerns *what* is to be equalized. We cannot rely on any particular account of what is valuable, because some reasonable people might not share it. As Rawls puts it,

> the government can no more act to maximize the fulfillment of citizens' rational preferences, or wants (as in utilitarianism), or to advance human excellence, or the values of perfection (as in perfectionism), than it can act to advance Catholicism or Protestantism, or any other religions. None of these views of the meaning, value, and purpose of human life, as specified by the corresponding comprehensive religious or philosophical doctrines, is affirmed by citizens generally, and so the pursuit of any one of them through basic institutions gives political society a sectarian character. (Rawls 1996: 179–80)

The most promising approach, therefore, is to focus on some measure of resources or capabilities that can be utilized for a wide range of ends. Just social institutions provide a background of liberty, opportunity, and resources with which individuals pursue their diverse ends. However, just institutions cannot guarantee individuals any particular level of success in their endeavors. There is a division of responsibility between the individual and society: "society, citizens as a collective body, accepts responsibility for maintaining the equal basic liberties and fair equality of opportunity, and for providing a fair share of the primary goods for all within this framework; while citizens as individuals and associations accept responsibility for revising and adjusting their ends and aspirations in view of the all-purpose means they can expect, given their present and foreseeable situation" (Rawls 1996: 189). The details of the principles need not detain us, and different conceptions can properly count as political conceptions. The important point is that all such conceptions will be broadly liberal. They will all guarantee a set of liberal civil and political rights, such as freedom of speech and assembly, religious liberty and the separation of church and state, and a right to democratic participation. They will also guarantee a fair share of resources to citizens with which to pursue their ends. There need not be a strict equality in the distribution of resources, but there will be some kind of constraint on permissible inequalities. (For Rawls's own principles, see Rawls 2001: part II; J. Mandle 2000b: ch. 2.)

After this summary of how political liberalism addresses the issue of social justice within a society, we are in a position to begin to consider whether a similar approach is appropriate in the case of global justice. Are the methods of justification that are appropriate when constructing principles of domestic justice also appropriate when constructing principles of global justice? I believe that they are. In the domestic case, the restrictions on acceptable justifications follow from two features: first, we are aiming to assess the coercive imposition of the basic structure; and second, we are doing so in conditions where people hold diverse comprehensive ethical and religious doctrines. With respect to the latter condition, certainly in the global context there is even greater diversity of comprehensive religions and ethical doctrines than there is in any single society. With respect to the former condition, the principles of global justice are to be used to guide the design of global institutions and the potentially coercive conduct of states with respect to one another. Now it is an important point, to which we will return, that the global basic structure differs from a domestic basic structure. In particular, the global order is not a state. I will argue in chapters 6 and 7 that this difference affects the content of the global principles of justice. The principles of global justice differ from the principles of domestic justice. But in both the domestic and the global case, the principles of justice aim at assessing the institutions and policies that can and should be coercively imposed in circumstances of deep diversity. In each case, therefore, our construction of principles should not be dependent on any single comprehensive ethical or religious doctrine. We should aim at providing a justification for the principles that does not depend on a single religion or comprehensive ethical theory.

3
Realism, Nationalism, and Cosmopolitanism

In this chapter, we will begin to consider whether the same principles that apply domestically within a society should also govern the relations among societies globally. We will look at the answers provided by three different doctrines. First, we will look at "foreign policy realism" (or "realism"), which holds that moral assessments ought to be limited to issues of domestic justice alone, and simply do not apply to international relations. Next, we will discuss (moderate) nationalism, which holds that considerations of justice do apply across borders, but that they are not as weighty as duties of justice owed to members of one's own nation. We will conclude this chapter by examining what I will call "strong cosmopolitanism," which holds that the same principles of justice that should be applied within a society ought also to be applied globally.

In its more extreme form, foreign policy realism holds that moral considerations simply do not apply when a country deals with other countries and foreigners. Rather, a country's only obligation in foreign policy is to pursue its own self-interest, principally through increasing its power. This position flourished in American foreign policy circles following World War II and through the Cold War. As one observer noted in 1986, "for the most part, discussions of foreign policy [in the United States] have been carried on, since 1945, in the language of political realism – that is, the language of power and interests rather than of ideals or norms" (Keohane 1986: 9). Although arguably, it has been losing ground in academic discussions of international relations recently, it remains a central, if no longer dominant, framework in policy circles.

On its surface, realism is perfectly straightforward. It is the view that Thucydides recorded in the so-called Melian dialogue which took place during the Peloponnesian War in the fifth century BCE.[1] The island of Melos was a colony of Sparta, which was at war with Athens. Although the Melians initially remained neutral, Athens sent a military force together with representatives to discuss the terms of the Melian surrender. The Athenian representatives were blunt and to the point, avoiding "noble phrases . . . about having the right to rule" and rejecting as irrelevant the argument that the Melians had remained neutral and done Athens no injury (Thucydides 1998: 295; bk V, para. 89). Against Melian pleas for justice, the Athenians simply pointed to their military superiority, insisting that justice was irrelevant when there was an imbalance in power, and claiming that all human beings "are under an innate compulsion to rule wherever empowered" (298; bk V, para. 105). Furthermore, the Athenians pointed out that the Melians should not expect assistance from Sparta, because while "in dealing with their own affairs and their local institutions, the Lacedaemonians [Spartans] are the greatest practitioners of virtue; where others are involved . . . they are the most striking example we know of men who regard what is agreeable as noble and what is expedient as just" (298; bk V, para. 105). The Melians concluded the dialogue by asking once again to be allowed to remain neutral, but the Athenians rejected this, attacked, and eventually conquered the island, "killed all of the grown men they captured, enslaved the children and women," and made it a colony of their own (301; bk V, para. 116).

Contemporary defenders of realism admire the unsentimental view expressed by the Athenians, as well as the view that the Athenians attribute to their enemy the Spartans: justice may be a virtue within a society, but it is simply irrelevant between nations, where each legitimately pursues its own narrow self-interest, independent of the interests of others and considerations of justice. According to the realists, the Melian pleas for justice *properly* carried no weight with the Athenians. Realists are given to apparently hard-nosed, uncompromising state-ments that express contempt for that naiveté of any view that relies on ethical considerations. Thus the American diplomat George Kennan wrote famously that it is a fundamental error to assume that "state behavior is a fit subject of moral judg-ment" (Kennan 1951: 100). In an interview conducted a few years before his death, he commented:

> I would like to see our government gradually withdraw from its public advocacy of democracy and human rights. Let me stress: I am speaking of governments, not private parties. If others in our country want to advocate democracy or human rights (whatever those terms mean), that's perfectly all right. But I don't think any such questions should enter into our diplomatic relations with other countries. (Ullman 1999: 6)

The political scientist most responsible for developing realism as an academic discipline in the mid-twentieth century was Hans Morgenthau, who characterized realism this way:

> The political realist maintains the autonomy of the political sphere, as the economist, the lawyer, the moralist maintain theirs. He thinks in terms of interest defined as power, as the economist thinks in terms of interest defined as wealth; the lawyer, of the conformity of action with legal rules; the moral-ist, of the conformity of action with moral principles. . . .
> The political realist is not unaware of the existence and relevance of standards of thought other than political ones. As political realist, he cannot but subordinate these other stand-ards to those of politics. And he parts company with other schools when they impose standards of thought appropriate to other spheres upon the political sphere. It is here that political realism takes issue with the "legalistic-moralistic" approach to international politics. (Morgenthau and Thompson 1985: 13–14)

In other words, international relations forms an autonomous sphere, behavior in which is properly governed by its own non-moral standards. Morgenthau argues that nations ought to pursue "the national interest" to the exclusion of all other con-siderations: "And, above all, remember always that it is not only a political necessity but also a moral duty for a nation to follow in its dealings with other nations but one guiding star, one standard for thought, one rule for action: The National Interest" (Morgenthau 1951: 242). Pursuit of the national interest, in turn, requires pursuit of power: "The main signpost that helps political realism find its way through the landscape of international politics is the concept of interest defined in terms of power" (Morgenthau and Thompson 1985: 5). Thus, realism holds that in international affairs the exclusive focus on the national interest is properly pursued through an expansion of power: "International politics, like all politics, is a struggle for power" (p. 31).

Any full assessment of the realist account of international relations will have to resolve a persistent ambiguity in its understanding of the ideas of the national interest and of power.[2] Here, I will assume that this can be done successfully. Typically, realists present their theory as an account of how international relations are actually conducted. As one historian of realism says, "As opposed to utopians, idealists, optimists, and reformers of every stripe, realists say they accept and understand the world as it is; this understanding provides the foundation for all their ideas" (Smith 1986: 1). Realists believe that they provide a more accurate account of the relations among nations than do moralists, who (supposedly) idealize these relations. Here is a typical statement from Morgenthau: "Writers have put forward moral precepts that statesmen and diplomats ought to take to heart in order to make relations between nations more peaceful and less anarchic. . . . But they have rarely asked themselves whether and to what extent such precepts, however desirable in themselves, actually determine the actions of men" (Morgenthau and Thompson 1985: 248). Morgenthau here shows an awareness of the distinction between a normative investigation into the principles and ideals that nations should strive for when interacting with others and the empirical historical investigation of the extent to which they have actually lived up to those ideals. He presents himself as pursuing a purely descriptive and dispassionate science, unswayed by the siren call of ideal moral principles.

But while realists are quick to accuse their opponents of assuming that nations will behave in accordance with some ideal principles, they typically assume without argument that they can deduce norms of behavior from descriptions of actual conduct. Mearsheimer, for example, is explicit that realism fills both roles: "It should be apparent from this discussion that offensive realism is mainly a descriptive theory. . . . But it is also a prescriptive theory" (Mearsheimer 2001: 11). Morgenthau himself also treated realism as both a descriptive and a normative theory. As one commentator puts it:

> Morgenthau explicitly acknowledged that the assumption of rationality was not descriptively accurate – indeed, one of his purposes was to instruct leaders in order to enable them to act more rationally – but he believed that it could be used as a baseline, which could be "tested against the actual facts" . . . Against the baseline provided by the theory's prediction, we can ask how "imperfections" caused by misperceptions, a lack of information, bargaining perversities, or even sheer irrationality could have made actual patterns of behavior diverge from our expectations. (Keohane 1986: 12)

There is nothing wrong with a social scientist presenting an "ideal type" that serves a useful purpose in organizing and clarifying our understanding of complex phenomena, even if it is not perfectly accurate descriptively. But to infer that actual cases that diverge from this ideal are somehow defective or faulty or "irrational" is to privilege the ideal with a normative status that needs to be earned from more than its (alleged) descriptive adequacy. If a country does not act as the theory predicts, we cannot straightaway conclude that the behavior was defective or irrational. Such a conclusion would require a normative defense of the ideal, and with this we move into explicitly moral territory (Moellendorf 2002: 145).

Why do realists move so quickly from a description of international relations in which countries pursue power and their narrow self-interest to a normative account in which it is appropriate for them to do so? When this is not simply an oversight, it is typically due to a specific view about the relationship between morality and law. This theory was developed most clearly in the work of Thomas Hobbes in the mid-seventeenth century. The thought is that in the absence of a strong central authority capable of enforcing its rules and judgment, there is no reason for individuals to constrain their pursuit of self-interest. As Hobbes put it: "Where there is no common power, there is no law; where no law, no injustice" (Hobbes [1660]

1994: 78; ch. 13, para. 13). Outside a commonwealth, in the state of nature, "every man has a right to everything, even to one another's body" (p. 80; ch. 14, para. 4). In this condition, it would simply be irrational and dangerous to limit oneself unilaterally: "if other men will not lay down their right as well as he, then there is no reason for anyone to divest himself of his; for that were to expose himself to prey (which no man is bound to), rather than to dispose himself to peace" (p. 80; ch. 14, para. 5). Hobbes concluded that remaining in this natural condition would be disastrous – peace is extremely valuable – and everyone therefore has a strong self-interested reason to establish or enter a commonwealth with a sovereign powerful enough to make and enforce laws.

Many realists follow Hobbes's lead and argue that the lack of a global state means that the international arena is in a condition of anarchy, analogous to the state of nature that Hobbes describes, leaving states in a "a posture of war" in relation to one another (Milner 1993). Since there is no powerful authority capable of enforcing international law, states have no reason to constrain their self-interested pursuits. Realists conclude from this that moral considerations do not apply, and that to suppose otherwise is to assume mistakenly that others will constrain their behavior. Morgenthau is explicit on this point: "There is a profound and neglected truth hidden in Hobbes's extreme dictum that the state creates morality as well as law and that there is neither morality nor law outside the state" (Morgenthau 1951: 34). Notice that if realists were to follow this Hobbesian logic to its conclusion, they would hold that the creation of a global state is a goal of the utmost urgency. Some realists, in fact, do take this step, although they quickly point out that such a goal is hopelessly utopian. According to his biographer, Christoph Frei, "As early as 1934 – and long before Hiroshima – Morgenthau pointed to the world state as a logical requirement, knowing full well that his postulate could not yet be realized: all preconditions 'are lacking in the world today.' Until the end of his life, he would hold on to this belief in the rational necessity of the world state, 'unattainable in our world, yet indispensable for the survival of that world' " (Frei 2001: 140–1). To choose another example, Mearsheimer writes that the "cycle of violence" of the twentieth century "will continue far into the new millennium. . . . This is a tragic situation, but there is no escaping it unless the states that make up the system agree to form a world government. Such a vast transformation is hardly a realistic prospect, however, so conflict and war are bound to continue as large and enduring features of world politics" (Mearsheimer 2001: p. xii).

There is a large literature concerning the extent to which the international order is analogous to Hobbes's state of nature. Some theorists argue, for example, that there is considerable overlap of interests among (at least many) states, while others point to the growth of international institutions, associations, and corporations as features that distinguish the international order from Hobbes's state of nature (Beitz 1999: 42–7; Grieco 1993a, 1993b). This literature has generated important criticisms of the descriptive adequacy of realism, but I will grant for the sake of argument that realists may provide a reasonably accurate descriptive account of the behavior of states. Still, their skeptical conclusion concerning principles of global justice does not follow, because the Hobbesian account of morality is inadequate. While I will argue below that political association changes our duties of justice in important ways, there remains a core of morality that is independent of political associations, and therefore applies globally even in the absence of a global state. That is, part of morality concerns our treatment of all persons, regardless of whether they share a common state that is powerful enough to enforce its laws.

When they attack morality, realists such as Morgenthau often take their opponent to be a fanatical moral crusader: "The immorality of a politically effective appeal to moral abstractions in foreign policy is consummated in the contemporary phenomenon of the moral crusade. . . . [The crusader] projects the national moral standards onto the international scene not only with the legitimate claim of reflecting the national interest, but with the politically and morally unfounded claim of providing moral standards for all mankind to conform to in concrete political action" (Morgenthau 1951: 36–7). Again and again, realists recoil from "moral excess" of the fanatical pursuit of allegedly "moral" goals that fails to recognize the human costs involved. This suggests that what ultimately lies at the heart of the normative claims of the realists is not a rejection of ethical considerations as such, but rather a rejection of a particular picture of morality – a rejection of the "moralizer" discussed in chapter 1. Their position is best understood as one concerning the *content* of morality, not the radical skepticism that sometimes characterizes their rhetoric. When they say that they are rejecting morality, in fact they are typically rejecting only an extremely skewed and inadequate picture of morality (M. Cohen 1984). As one defender of the realist tradition writes, "despite their apparent claim that the overt pursuit of morality should have no place in foreign policy, a moral vision informs the entire realist approach" (Smith 1986: 21–2). This appears to be true of George Kennan, whose attitudes were formed in reaction to what one theorist has called the "spasm of crusading idealism" that led the United States into World War I and the willingness of some to force a nuclear confrontation with the Soviet Union after World War II (Steel 2004: 8). Michael Smith claims that, "Despite his protestations of realism and his recommendations for a policy of national interest, Kennan remains a formidable adherent of a traditional morality" (Smith 1986: 166). This is also true of Morgenthau, who complained bitterly in private letters that his work was misunderstood and that he was not opposed to morality (Frei 2001: esp. 204, 213). He also devoted himself to what could only be called international moral causes, such as serving as chairman of the Academic Committee on Soviet Jewry (p. 170).

What is needed, therefore, is an account of justice that does not force individuals or societies to become "prey" when others are unwilling to reciprocate, and that recognizes that sometimes one must forgo morally admirable ends when the only available means have an unacceptably high moral cost. If we reject the radical skepticism that the realists sometimes express, but accept the need for a subtle, non-moralizing account of global justice, there remains an immense range of possible positions. Moral considerations should count in a country's foreign policy deliberations, but should the interests of foreigners receive the same consideration and weight that we give to our fellow nationals? Nationalists say that we should give priority to our co-nationals, while (strong) cosmopolitans say that everyone's interests should be given equal weight.

Nationalism is a family of extremely diverse phenomena that can be approached from a number of distinct perspectives. One can ask interesting questions about its history, sociology, and psychology, for example. Here, we will consider nationalism only insofar as it helps us to determine which principles of international justice to endorse and, specifically, whether the principles that apply to international relations differ from domestic principles. To begin, we must introduce two distinctions. First, consider the difference between particularistic and universalistic nationalism (Pogge 2002: 119; cf. D. Miller 1995: 9). *Particularistic nationalism* is the thesis that one particular nation or people – for example, the Japanese or the Greek or the Argentinian people – are specially chosen and valuable from the moral point of view itself. *Generalized nationalism*, in contrast, says that each individual properly has a morally weighty attachment to his or her nation, whatever it happens to be. On this view, the moral point of view itself does not single out any particular nation for special treatment; rather, it authorizes individuals to do so themselves, based on their own identification. I will follow most contemporary theories of nationalism and focus exclusively on generalized nationalism. As Thomas Pogge observes, dismissing all forms of particularistic nationalism, "On account of the chauvinist, often racist, distinctions such views invoke, they are not worth serious moral discussion" (Pogge 2002: 119). It is worth noting, however, that historically particularistic nationalism has often had the most dramatic political influence.

The second fundamental distinction concerns the difference between a nation and a state. Let us define a state as a political entity containing a sovereign system of law. In the modern context, states are territorial. Although borders may be disputed, and legitimacy challenged, states claim the right to rule over a geographic territory. The idea of a nation is much more difficult to define. What distinguishes a nation from some other group of people? Almost all commentators agree that some degree of subjective identification and mutual recognition are necessary, if not sufficient, for a group to constitute a nation. In order for there to be a French nation, for example, people must identify themselves and one another as French. The sociologist Craig Calhoun captures this requirement when he writes: "Recognition as a nation clearly requires social solidarity – some level of integration among the members of the ostensible nation, and collective identity – the recognition of the whole by its members, and a sense of individual self that includes membership in the whole" (Calhoun 1997: 4).

On what grounds do individuals recognize co-nationals and distinguish them from foreigners? Nations have relied on many different features to ground their identification and to distinguish members from foreigners. In the mid-nineteenth century, John Stuart Mill observed that the "feeling of nationality may have been generated by various causes," and after listing several common factors such as race, common descent, language, and religion, he wrote: "None of these circumstances however are either indispensable, or necessarily sufficient by themselves" (Mill [1861] 1991: 427; ch. 16, para. 1; cf. Weber [1922] 1946: 172). As one contemporary critic of nationalism observes, "there is no limit in principle to the kind of traits that can underlie national(ist) identification: color of skin, dietary or sexual habits, and who knows what else might one day play a legitimate role in rallying together a group of people demanding recognition as a nation" (Miščević 2001: 11–12). But if national identification is so open-ended, what distinguishes it from other forms of social identification?

First, nations are characterized by a common culture, which itself may be manifest in various ways. As the philosophers Avishai Margalit and Joseph Raz put it, a nation has

> a common character and a common culture that encompass many, varied and important aspects of life, a culture that defines or marks a variety of forms or styles of life, types of activities, occupations, pursuits, and relationships. With national groups we expect to find national cuisines, distinctive architectural styles, a common language, distinctive literary and artistic traditions, national music, customs, dress, ceremonies and holidays, etc. None of these is necessary. They are but typical examples of the features that characterize peoples and other groups that are serious candidates for the right to self-determination. They have pervasive cultures, and their identity is determined at least in part by their culture. They possess cultural traditions that penetrate beyond a single or a few areas of human life, and display themselves in a whole range of areas, including many which are of great importance

for the well-being of individuals. (Margalit and Raz 1990: 443–4; cf. D. Miller 1995: 25–6)

Since a national culture is pervasive, individuals born into and socialized in a nation will typically "acquire the group culture, [and] will be marked by its character. Their tastes and their options will be affected by that culture to a significant degree." Although it may be possible for people to "shed their previous culture" and "acquire a new one," this is "a painful and slow process, success in which is rarely complete" (Margalit and Raz 1990: 444). Notice that different elements, not one of which is necessary, may go into making such a pervasive culture. This preserves Mill's insight that different nationalities may ground their identification in different social and cultural features.

The second element that distinguishes national identities from other forms of social identification is that nations have a political dimension. Again, Mill had the crucial insight when he suggested that people constitute a nation when "they are united among themselves by common sympathies . . . which make them co-operate with each other more willingly than with other people, desire to be under the same government, and desire that it should be government by themselves or a portion of themselves, exclusively" (Mill [1861] 1991: 427; ch. 16, para. 1; cf. Weber [1922] 1946: 176). Or, as David Miller writes: " 'nation' must refer to a community of people with an *aspiration* to be politically self-determining" (D. Miller 1995: 19). Typically, this is manifested in an aspiration to form (or to maintain) a state, yet in the case of certain multi-national states something less than full independence, such as special recognition, or some degree of autonomy, or participation within a confederated structure, may be sufficient.

In order to achieve a pervasive culture and to have a plausible aspiration to political self-rule, a nation must be large-scale and anonymous, rather than "face-to-face." In the celebrated phrase of Benedict Anderson, a nation is an *imagined community*: "It is *imagined* because the members of even the smallest nation will never know most of their fellow-members, meet them, or even hear of them, yet in the minds of each lives the image of their communion. . . . [I]t is imagined as a *community*, because, regardless of the actual inequality and exploitation that may prevail in each, the nation is always conceived as a deep, horizontal comradeship" (Anderson 1991: 6–7). So, members of a nation share a pervasive or comprehensive culture that affects many areas of their lives and self-conceptions, and may include such things as language, religion, values, daily habits, tastes, and preferences. In addition, membership in a nation will typically form an important part of an individual's self-conception and identity, and there will usually be a solidaristic bond with co-nationals, even though the vast majority are not known personally. And finally, a nation has a political element, since it aspires to political self-determination.[3]

The distinction introduced here between nations and states is sometimes obscured by the assumption that modern states simply *are* nation-states, rather than territorial states, or that nation-states can easily be formed, perhaps through some minor redrawing of borders. But given the fact that modern states are territorial, while nations are a matter of identification, recognition, and culture, it is no surprise that the two often fail to correspond. As Allen Buchanan observes, "states and comprehensive cultures . . . are not in one-to-one correspondence. Virtually every existing state (Iceland may be an exception) contains more than one such group" (Buchanan 2004: 178). Not all comprehensive cultural groups are *nations*, since they do not all have political aspirations, but many do, and therefore there are many multinational states, including Belgium, Canada, and China, as well as the former Soviet Union, the former Yugoslavia, and the historical empires of Great Britain and the Ottoman caliphate. *Nationalism*, according to one common definition, is the "political principle, which holds that the political and the national unit should be congruent" (Gellner 1983: 1). It is important to stress that this is a normative position – that state borders *ought* to be drawn or redrawn to achieve congruence between states and nations. We will discuss the issue of secession in chapter 6, but for now the important point is simply the moral significance that nationalists attribute to nationality. Nationalists typically infer from this moral significance that moral obligations to our co-nationals should take priority over moral obligations to foreigners. Nationalists make several arguments in support of this moral priority, and we will consider the two most common ones.

The first is what I will call the "efficiency argument," and is illustrated clearly by Robert Goodin. The idea is to begin with a moral universalistic position that at a fundamental level recognizes only " 'general duties' that we have toward other people, merely because they are people" (Goodin 1988: 663; cf. Nussbaum 1996: 135–6). However, we can then derive "special obligations" to "our fellow countrymen," because a system in which particular individuals are assigned particular responsibilities is often more efficient than if everyone attempts to discharge general duties toward all others. Consider, as an analogy, the allocation of responsibility in a hospital: "hospital patients are better cared for by being assigned to particular doctors rather than having all the hospital's doctors devote one nth of their time to each of the hospital's n patients" (Goodin 1988: 681). Thus, for Goodin, "Special responsibilities are, on my account, assigned merely as an administrative device for discharging our general duties more efficiently" (p. 685).

I am not convinced that all special responsibilities can be generated in this way. But even if we accept the efficiency argument, there are two implications noted by Goodin that are worth emphasizing. First, the efficiency argument does not attribute to national identity any *fundamental* moral significance. As Goodin points out, on this view, "it turns out that 'our fellow countrymen' are not so very special after all" (p. 679). Second, given the extreme inequality in the world today (to be discussed in chapter 7), if people give priority to their co-nationals, the poorest nations will be unable to provide for their members, while rich nations will be relieved of the burden of assisting the poor. Given the current distribution of wealth in the world, assigning a high priority to co-nationals would hinder rather than enhance our ability to fulfill our general obligations. Goodin recognizes this, and concludes his argument by asserting that "In the present world system, it is often – perhaps ordinarily – wrong to give priority to the claims of our compatriots" (p. 686). Given the current extent and nature of global inequality, nationalists can gain little support from the efficiency argument.

An alternative strategy for defending the moral priority of co-nationals is to argue that identification with a nation is analogous to identification with one's family. Just as many people believe that individuals have special obligations to their family members (and that they are not derived via the efficiency argument from general obligations), so too, nationalists argue, individuals have special obligations to co-nationals. Of course, belonging to the same nation as someone else is not literally the same as being members of the same family. After all, as we have seen, nations are not face-to-face communities. Still, the strongly felt identifications that many people have with their co-nationals are taken by some theorists to ground special moral obligations. Yael Tamir, for example, writes: "our obligation to help fellow members derives from a shared sense of membership" (Tamir 1993: 102). And on David Miller's account, "Principles of distributive justice . . . do indeed have a restricted scope, but the limits are not set by the bounds of a co-operative practice for mutual advantage; rather they are set by the bounds of a community whose members recognize one another as belonging to that community" (D. Miller 1998b: 278).

Liberal nationalists such as Yael Tamir and David Miller are willing to grant that the special moral concern that we owe to our co-nationals is compatible with a core commitment to universal human rights, and therefore that some important moral obligations extend beyond national boundaries. Miller is explicit on this point: "The duties we owe to our fellow-nationals are different from, and more extensive than, the duties we owe to human beings as such. This is not to say that we owe *no* duties to humans as such" (D. Miller 1995: 11). Miller distinguishes non-comparative principles, such as the protection of basic rights, from comparative principles, such as those concerned to limit inequalities of wealth and resources. This allows him to argue that "*comparative* principles of justice operate only within national boundaries, while noncomparative principles may also operate across them" (D. Miller 1998a: 171). More specifically, "there is nothing unjust about international inequalities as such" (p. 179). For Miller, the more demanding egalitarian principles of distributive justice apply only among individuals who view themselves as part of a nation.

Strong cosmopolitans object to even this more modest priority for co-nationals. They hold that from a moral point of view every human being should be treated as an equal, regardless of nationality or citizenship. As Charles Jones explains, the cosmopolitan standpoint is "impartial, universal, individualist, and egalitarian" (C. Jones 1999: 15). At a fundamental moral level, all individuals are to be treated as equals, regardless of nationality. Within this broad approach, however, there are important differences. Some argue, for example, that giving priority to members of one's nation is no better than racism (Gomberg 1990) or that it is an expression of "bad faith" (Keller 2005). More extreme cosmopolitans argue that we have an obligation to work toward the elimination of nations and national identification altogether. Sometimes as part of a project of reducing the importance of national identities, cosmopolitans (and, as we have seen, even some realists) argue for the creation of a world state, or at least an increase in the power of international political structures. Other cosmopolitans, however, support strengthened international political institutions without the elimination of national attachments and loyalties. One way to attempt to combine these commitments is through the efficiency argument endorsed by Goodin, according to which we have special obligations to our co-nationals if, but only if, such a system contributes to the overall achievement of a cosmopolitan system of value. A more moderate form of cosmopolitanism holds that while national identification is not objectionable in itself, and may even be a source of moral obligations, these additional obligations must remain within the limits imposed by cosmopolitan principles of justice. As Jones puts it: "It can be morally permissible, even required, that one be patriotic and loyal to one's country, but such permissions and requirements can never override the demands of impartial justice" (C. Jones 1999: 134). It is important to remember that there are moral obligations beyond the requirements of justice. The thought is that various local attachments may generate some of these additional moral obligations, but that they are not the (fundamental) source of any obligations of justice (Moellendorf 2002: 35).

To see the problem with attempting to ground obligations of justice in national identity, recall that when we justify principles of justice, we must present arguments that could be acceptable to reasonable people who do not share a single religion or comprehensive system of values. Just as we must reject principles of justice that depend on the truth of some particular religion, so too we must reject principles that depend on the truth of particularistic nationalism – the assumption that members of some particular nation are specially privileged from the moral point of view. But we also must reject principles of justice that depend on the truth of generalized nationalism – the assumption that everyone has a morally weighty identification with his or her nation. While some people take their national identity to be fundamental, not all do. Some people will take their religious or professional or ethnic or political identification to be fundamental, while many others would be reluctant to take any one affiliation or identity to necessarily override all others in the case of conflicts. Although some moral obligations may be grounded in particular relationships and identifications, principles of justice cannot be so grounded without undermining their capacity to adjudicate conflicts among all reasonable people (Buchanan 1998).

I agree with the strong cosmopolitans that any attempt to ground duties of justice in subjective identification will fail. We do not have any stronger obligations of justice toward our co-nationals (as such) than toward anyone else. But, unlike the strong cosmopolitans, I believe that citizenship – that is, political membership in a state (rather than a nation) – can make a fundamental difference from the point of view of justice. Indeed, I will follow David Miller in holding that non-comparative principles apply at a global level, but depart from him when I claim that the egalitarian, comparative principles apply not within a nation (as he claims),[4] but within a state. I will defend this view in chapters 6 and 7. But before we can see what difference shared political institutions make, we must establish the basic cosmopolitan duties of justice that apply to all. Thus, in the next two chapters I will provide an account of basic human rights.

4
Human Rights

In this chapter I will present an account of basic human rights that is developed for use in a theory of global justice. The core human rights I will discuss must be respected by all, and are owed to all human beings in the words of the Universal Declaration of Human Rights, "without discrimination of any kind, such as race, colour, sex, language, religion, political or other opinion, national or social origin, property, birth or other status" (United Nations 1948b: article 2). Because the account of rights presented here is shaped by the specific role they are to play in a theory of global justice, they are more limited in content and are given a different defense than would be appropriate in other contexts and for other purposes. In keeping with a political conception of justice, I will make no attempt to develop a comprehensive ethical theory based on rights. Even the properly celebrated Universal Declaration of Human Rights, the history of which we will examine in chapter 5, contains a more extensive list of rights than I will defend, although many of its more specific rights fall under the more general headings I present. My discussion, tailored for a specific purpose, remains agnostic concerning other possible roles.

As I will understand the concept, to claim that something is a basic human right is to claim that there should be a high level of social protection given to securing the right's content against standard violations and threats.[1] To the extent possible, our basic social institutions should be designed to protect the content – the substance – of our basic human rights. Obviously, to claim that something is a basic human right is to make a moral claim. Making such a claim is typically a way of establishing a basis for evaluating social practices, policies, laws, or institutions. The fact that a society fails to protect or even sometimes violates some purported basic right does not refute the existence of that right. On the contrary, if we decide that a society does not adequately protect some right, this is often the basis for a powerful condemnation of its institutions or policies. What follows from such a condemnation, and what moral requirements are placed on individuals when a basic human right is violated, are further questions. But basic human rights generate a strong moral duty on societies, and therefore on the individuals who support and can influence those societies, to establish structures and policies to protect them. They typically have priority over other, possibly competing moral concerns.

Ronald Dworkin captures this priority of the protection of rights over other considerations by saying that rights should be considered "trumps" (Dworkin 1977: p. xi; cf. Dworkin 1984). Although in some ways useful, speaking of "rights as trumps" is liable to generate two misunderstandings. First, it is sometimes assumed that to speak of trumps implies that rights are absolute, and that no considerations could ever be sufficient to justify violating a right. This is not Dworkin's position, and for most if not all rights it would be unreasonable. According to Dworkin, what is characteristic of a right is only that it has "a certain threshold weight against collective goals in general . . . for example, it cannot be defeated by appeal to any of the ordinary routine goals of political administration, but only by a goal of special urgency" (Dworkin 1977: 92). This leaves open exactly how much weight they are to be given, but Dworkin is explicit that they are not necessarily absolute over all other concerns: "Rights may also be less than absolute; one principle might have to yield to another, or even to an urgent policy with which it competes on particular facts" (ibid.).

The second misunderstanding is related. Sometimes it is assumed that when human rights are invoked, there is no longer any room for debate, perhaps because they are assumed to have a foundational status or to be metaphysically distinct from other more ordinary concerns (Ignatieff 2001). When Dworkin introduces his account, he says that it departs from rival accounts precisely because it "does not suppose that rights have some special metaphysical character" (Dworkin 1977: p. xi). The important point for us here is that when we call something a basic human right, we must be able to defend that claim. Such defenses are open to challenge and are subject to debate. We must explain why a high level of social protection is required for some goods and not others. Furthermore, if two (purported) rights conflict, this need not result in a moral stalemate. When such a conflict emerges, we must make explicit the grounds for the rights, so that the relative strengths of the claims can be assessed.

Although social institutions and policies should be designed to give a high level of protection to basic rights, this protection cannot be absolute. Henry Shue is right that it would be an "absurd standard" to insist that "a right has been fulfilled only if it is impossible for anyone to be deprived of it or only if no one is ever deprived of it. The standard can only be some reasonable level of guarantee" (Shue 1996: 17; cf. Scanlon 2003: 116). When this level of social protection is achieved, the right is secured. A right not to be murdered, for example, certainly requires that the government not itself engage in murder. It also requires that the government take adequate steps to prevent individuals from committing murder. But once these steps have been taken, the right is secured for all, even if a small number of random acts of violence continue to occur (Pogge 2002: 38). Conversely, if there is inadequate protection, a right is not secure, even if through good fortune its substance is not violated. What counts as adequate protection will depend among other things on the prevalence and nature of the threats in a particular society. Although creating a law is often a key tool in protecting basic rights, it is neither necessary nor sufficient. Simply passing a law against murder, for example, would not be adequate if it is not effectively enforced.

To claim that something is a basic human right is to do more than simply claim that enjoying the substance of that right would be good. It is to make a moral *demand*, specifically a demand for a high level of social protection against certain standard threats. When a basic human right exists, it generates a duty on all other individuals to respect the substance of that right. A right not to be murdered, for example, generates a duty on all individuals not to commit murder. But our focus here is not on individual duties that are generated directly in this way, but rather on duties that are mediated by social institutions. Only social institutions can provide adequate protection, especially for the weak and vulnerable (Shue 1996: 16). Therefore, as Pogge observes, "We should conceive human rights primarily as claims on coercive social institutions and secondarily as claims against those who uphold such institutions" (Pogge 2002: 44–5). One implication of this understanding of basic human rights is that they may or may not correspond to the idea of natural rights, understood as the rights that individuals have outside society or in a state of nature.

Basic human rights generate duties on everyone who is in a position to influence the relevant social institutions, although these duties are not necessarily equally demanding for all. Allen Buchanan links the idea of basic rights to what he calls the "Natural Duty of Justice" this way: "each of us – independently of which institutions we find ourselves in or the special commitments we have undertaken – has a limited moral obligation to help ensure that all persons have access to institutions that protect their basic rights" (Buchanan 2004: 12). This duty of justice requires that we do what we can to help create and maintain institutions that secure basic human rights. Typically, our ability to do this will be greatest in the case of our own society. But when we have the ability to assist anyone in securing their basic human rights, and we can do this without making excessive sacrifices, we have a duty to do so. The strength of this duty, and the extent of the sacrifices required, may vary depending on many contingent features of the particular case.

Social institutions are human creations. In Rawls's words, "The social system is not an unchangeable order beyond human control but a pattern of human action" (Rawls 1999a: 88; cf. Buchanan 2004: 75). Since they are the product of human behavior, we can ask whether institutions are just or unjust and how they should be changed, if at all. People are responsible, both individually and collectively, for ensuring that institutions are just and adequately protect basic human rights. Typically, responsibility for institutions is widely dispersed, since no particular individual has complete control over them, and an unjust institution may persist simply because of the acquiescence of participants who see no realistic alternative. Different people, of course, may be more or less responsible for the injustice of a particular institution. And just as, other things being equal, those who can assist in the creation of just institutions without excessive costs to themselves have a greater obligation to do so than those for whom it would require a great sacrifice, so too, other things being equal, those individuals who have actively created or supported unjust institutions have a greater responsibility to change them than do those who have passively accepted them.

Sometimes this contrast is presented as a difference between negative and positive duties. A negative duty prohibits an individual from undertaking some action, while a positive duty requires that some action be performed. An individual violates a negative duty, then, when she actively does something that is impermissible. By contrast, she may be in violation of a positive duty when she simply does nothing and fails to engage in some required activity. It is widely assumed that actively doing something bad (say, committing a murder) is worse than failing to prevent an equivalent bad from happening (say, by failing to rescue a murder victim), and so a violation of a negative duty is a more severe wrong than the violation of a corresponding positive duty. I do not want to challenge the intuition behind this belief, but simply to observe that the sharp contrast between negative and positive duties is often inadequate when actions are mediated through social institutions.

To illustrate some of the complexities involved in institutional responsibility, consider the following four cases in which basic human rights are denied (cf. Pogge 2002: 41–2). First, at one extreme, is a totalitarian state that systematically terrorizes its population through murder and torture. Government officials who order and carry out such policies are certainly engaged in grossly immoral behavior. They are violating a strong negative duty. The soldiers who carry out these acts share the moral blame, but the main responsibility falls with the political and military leaders who devise the policies and issue the orders. By contrast, the citizens of such a society may bear little responsibility for these violations. They may primarily be victims, with few if any opportunities to resist. A second example is a society in which the government does not itself carry out such acts, but allows private death squads to engage in them without interference. Perhaps there are even laws on the books that prohibit such activities, but government officials turn a blind eye when the laws are violated. In such a case, the moral failure on the part of government officials shares some features with a violation of positive duty, since the officials are not carrying out the murders and tortures themselves, but are merely failing to take the active steps, such as enforcing the law, that would be necessary to prevent the severe harms. Still, because the government is failing to ensure a sufficient level of protection, it is appropriate to say that officials bear partial responsibility for the violation of human rights. In a third society, once again death squads terrorize the population through random murders and torture. Here, however, while the government is fully committed to eradicating this threat, the death squads are well funded, and the government suffers from a lack of resources. Despite enjoying popular support in its fight, the government is largely unable to contain the threat. Here again, I think we would want to say that we have a case of human rights violations, since the social structure is failing to provide adequate protection for the citizens. But in this case responsibility for these violations falls exclusively on the shoulders of the death squads themselves, and if the government officials are doing all they can to contain the violations, they should not be blamed, even if they are largely unsuccessful in providing security. Notice that in these cases the source of the threat differs. In the first case, the government deliberately targets individuals, while in the third it aims to protect them, even though it is ineffective in doing so. As we will see, foreigners seeking to assist in the protection of basic human rights must be sensitive to these differences. While pressure may be appropriate in one case, the other requires assistance.

Consider now a final example, in which the government is fully accountable to the majority through free and democratic elections. A particular region in this society is populated by an ethnic minority, and in that territory private death squads target the minority and operate with impunity. The government could take action to crack down on the terror squads, but the majority believes that since they are largely confined to a particular region, doing so is not a priority. It is not that the majority actively supports the death squads. The latter simply do not register as a major concern for most people, and the government reflects this indifference. Once again, we have a case of human rights violations, since the basic structure is not effectively protecting the basic human rights of all. In this case, responsibility for the violations falls not only on the death squads and the government officials, but is shared by the population as a whole. It seems to me that in this case, the traditional distinction between negative and positive duties is inadequate. On the one hand, ordinary citizens are certainly not engaged in murder. Indeed, even the government officials have not given such orders. As in the second case, the government officials and citizens generally are simply allowing the violations to occur, and this makes it look as though there is a violation of merely a positive duty – a failure to prevent harm. On the other hand, the social structure itself is being coercively imposed on the territory. Since the social structure is coercively imposed, and since it is unjust because it fails to afford adequate protection to basic human rights, this makes it appear much closer to a violation of a negative duty. Again: the moral violations of these citizens share some features with negative duties (since the inadequate social structure and governmental policies that they support are being coercively imposed on all), but also some features with positive duties (since they and their government are merely allowing the violations to occur). I see no reason to force a complicated case such as this into either mold. Ultimately, the issue is not the classification of a violation as negative or positive, but rather the assessment of the strength of reasons that individuals and groups have to act in a way to prevent the violation. This depends on the degree of responsibility for bringing about the violation (including responsibility mediated through coercively imposed social institutions) and the sacrifices that would be necessary to prevent the violations.

With this understanding of basic human rights, we can now discuss their content. To identify the content of the basic human rights, we must determine, as Buchanan puts it, which "interests are so important for human flourishing that the most basic institutions should be designed so as to protect them" (Buchanan 2004: 66). Since we will be using the idea of human rights to determine what global justice requires, our argument should not depend on any particular conception of human flourishing or comprehensive ethical or religious doctrine. It must be able to command the free allegiance of people who hold widely different views about these fundamental matters. As Abdullahi Ahmed An-Na'Im, himself a defender of human rights from a Muslim perspective, argues:

> If international standards of human rights are to be implemented in a manner consistent with their own rationale, the people (who are to implement these standards) must perceive the concept of human rights and its content as their own. To be committed to carrying out human rights standards, people must hold these standards as emanating from their worldview and values, not imposed on them by outsiders. (An-Na'Im 1992: 431)

An-Na'Im is right that human rights must be compatible with people's broader moral and cultural outlooks. But in a context of diversity, the justification of rights cannot be dependent on any single comprehensive doctrine. To tie human rights exclusively to a single, ultimate foundation would be to undermine the possibility of justifying them to those who hold a different comprehensive doctrine. As part of the process of writing the Universal Declaration of Human Rights, to be discussed in chapter 5, UNESCO (the United Nations Educational, Scientific and Cultural Organization) investigated how human rights were understood and regarded in many different cultural, religious, and intellectual traditions. In a volume reporting many of their findings, Jacques Maritain tells the following story: "It is related that at one of the meetings of a UNESCO National Commission where human rights were being discussed, someone expressed astonishment that certain champions of violently opposed ideologies had agreed on a list of those rights. 'Yes,' they said, 'we agree about the rights *but on condition that no one asks us why*' " (Maritain 1949: 9). This is an excellent illustration of what Jack Donnelly, following Rawls, calls "an overlapping consensus on international human rights" (Donnelly 2003: 40).[2]

One strategy to accomplish this would be to attempt to find some features of human flourishing that are shared by all reasonable comprehensive doctrines. An alternative strategy, and one that I believe is more promising, is to attempt to find things that all reasonable doctrines hold would *ruin* a life. As Michael Ignatieff observes, "people from different cultures may continue to disagree about what is good, but nevertheless agree about what is insufferably, unarguably wrong" (Ignatieff 2001: 4; cf. Buchanan 2004: 128; Hampshire 1989: 90). Following this approach, I now propose the following list of basic human rights:

1   rights associated with physical security – including the right not to be murdered, tortured, or enslaved, as well as to bodily integrity;
2   basic rights of due process and the rule of law – including prohibition of arbitrary arrest and imprisonment; a right to an impartial hearing when one is accused of a crime, and formal equality before the law;
3   a right to political participation – that is, a right to participate in the process of making the laws that apply to one, either directly or indirectly by selecting representatives; this also entails a right to free (political) speech and association;
4   basic liberties of conscience, expression, and association – including freedom to worship as one chooses (if one chooses) and to change religious affiliation; at least a minimal degree of freedom of speech (in one's own language); freedom to form peaceful associations, both political and personal, including marriage; and a right to emigrate;[3]
5   the right to a minimally adequate share of resources – including adequately nutritious food, clean water, and basic health care; and the ability to control personal property;
6   a right to a basic education – including literacy and free access to information.

Regardless of the specific account of flourishing that one endorses, the denial of any of these would (at a minimum) significantly undermine one's prospects of living a satisfactory life.

Before examining each of these in more detail, let me emphasize that the precise level of social protection that is required for these rights will vary. This is because the threats against the substance of these rights differ in different circumstances, and also because the resources that a society can deploy for their protection varies. For example, the extent and nature of the health care that a society must provide in order adequately to protect the fifth basic human right will depend on factors such as the wealth of the society, the kinds of threats to the health of citizens that are common, the level of technology available to them, along with much else. There is no assumption that some single institutional structure is best to protect the substance of these rights in all circumstances. Michael Freeman emphasizes this point when he writes: "Human-rights principles are abstract and general, but must always be implemented in complex, particular situations. . . . The implementation of human rights, therefore, cannot be derived directly from international texts, but must be mediated by judgements about particular local circumstances, including local cultures" (Freeman 2002: 109). It often makes sense to have local political institutions provide these further specifications and applications, although these judgments are not, and should not be, treated as infallible (Freeman 2002: 109; Buchanan 2004: 180–90).

Little commentary, I think, is necessary concerning the right to physical security. It is perfectly obvious that murder, torture, enslavement, and rape are very severe harms, no matter what specific religion or comprehensive ethical doctrine and view of the good life one holds. Furthermore, living in a society that does not adequately secure one from these threats is itself a serious impediment to living a good life. Even if an individual is not raped, for example, the fact that she does not have protection against such a threat leaves her vulnerable and liable to be intimidated, coerced, and abused in other ways. It is clearly not enough for the government to refrain from itself engaging in such violations. It must actively take steps to prevent others from engaging in them as well, and thereby to secure citizens against otherwise credible threats. As Henry Shue writes, "A demand for physical security is not normally a demand simply to be left alone, but a demand to be protected against harm. It is a demand for positive action, or, in the words of our initial account of a right, a demand for social guarantees against at least the standard threats" (Shue 1996: 38–9). The law is often a necessary tool against such abuses, but as we have seen, by itself it is not sufficient, since resources must be deployed to enforce the law and to prevent violations.

The deployment of powers to enforce the law itself involves risk, and there must be clear and substantial institutional constraints on those who are granted such powers. The ideal of the rule of law captures the most basic of these constraints. Officials empowered to arrest and punish in the name of the state must do so only on the basis of public laws that are administered impartially and fairly. The specific institutional mechanisms to ensure this may vary, but the basic rights of due process and formal equality before the law must be secured. If officials are able to make arbitrary arrests or to impose punishments with no possible appeal, we have a system not of law, but of illegitimate power that leaves people vulnerable to the very abuse from which they seek protection. This is true even if the officials who happen to be in power are generally benevolent. The fact that people depend on the whim of their rulers leaves them exposed, and their basic human rights cannot be said to be protected, even if the content of those rights happens not to be violated. Shue makes the point this way: "What is missing that keeps people under the ideally enlightened despot . . . from enjoying rights . . . is social institutions for demanding the fulfillment of the correlative duties, especially the duty to provide one vital form of protection: protection against deprivation by the government itself, if it should become less enlightened and less benevolent" (Shue 1996: 76).

The same argument supports a basic right to political participation. It is not only the application and enforcement of the law that generates serious risks of abuse. The process through which laws are made can also be corrupt, so there must be institutional mechanisms that allow the people to whom the law applies to influence its creation. I will argue below that this is a necessary requirement for a legitimate political order and legitimate law. One obvious mechanism is a democratic legislature, based on the principle of "one person, one vote." But, as we will see below, this is not the only possibility. Whatever the mechanism, however, it must allow individuals to be able freely to form and to register their judgments about laws and policies, and this requires a measure of freedom of speech – at least of political speech.

Furthermore, government officials have an obligation to take such challenges seriously and to offer public replies framed in terms of their understanding of the general good. If these requirements are not met, there is not an adequate check on the power of the law-makers. And without such a constraint, the institutional structure does not provide a sufficient guarantee that the content of the other basic rights will be protected. Again, this is not to say that any society without a right to political participation will inevitably degenerate into a tyranny in which torture and murder are common. But, as we have seen, respecting a right requires that society provide adequate structural guarantees against harms, and a paternalistic society that does not allow political participation depends too heavily on the arbitrary discretion of the rulers. In such a society, basic human rights are not adequately protected, even if for a time their content is not violated.

This instrumental justification for a right to political participation should not be taken to disparage the intrinsic value of a political life. For some, a flourishing life requires active participation in the political life of their community, but others will disagree. The argument given here remains agnostic on this issue, but holds that the right to political participation is necessary in order to secure protection for all ways of life. To say that there is a human right to political participation does not imply that there is a duty to participate. Shue's example generalizes: "That I have a right to freedom of movement, for instance, does not mean that I must constantly or, for that matter, ever move, if I do not wish to" (Shue 1996: 73). Finally, notice that this account entails more than a merely *formal* right to participation. There must be a genuine opportunity and ability to participate in and influence the political decisions of one's society. It is not only formal exclusion that undermines this right. If an individual is unable to get to the voting booth or to read the candidates' names once there, her right to participation is not being secured effectively.

Liberty of conscience, as I conceive it in this context, should be understood broadly. That is, it should protect not only worship and membership in traditional religions, but a broader range of sincerely held doctrines and practices. Although broad, the degree of protection need not be as deep as liberal principles of domestic justice require. For example, although the worst forms of religious persecution are ruled out, this basic human right does not rule out all forms of discrimination – even official discrimination. If an official is denied a position of high political authority on religious grounds, this would be unjust according to liberal principles of domestic justice, but it would not violate any basic human rights. This is for the simple reason that such discrimination, although perhaps unjust, does not rise to the level that would be likely to ruin a life (absent very special circumstances). As Buchanan observes, "the notion of a decent human life does not mandate anything so strong as strict equality of treatment. . . . Though there will be borderline cases, we can and do distinguish between less damaging forms of inequality that qualify as discrimination and those that constitute persecution, and between more and less damaging forms of discrimination as well" (Buchanan 2004: 130).

On the other hand, individuals must be protected from persecution on the basis of their beliefs, and there must be no formal prohibition on entering or leaving a religion, association, or marriage. When an individual is forced to lead a life contrary to his or her conscience and deepest held values, there is little hope of that life being satisfactory. Will Kymlicka argues that a necessary but not sufficient condition for a life to be a good one is that it is lived "from the inside," that is, in accordance with the values and ideals endorsed by that person: "no life goes better by being led from the outside according to values the person does not endorse. My life only goes better if I am leading it from the inside, according to my beliefs about value" (Kymlicka 1990: 203–4). There is no need to deny that some values and ideals may be better than others. The point is simply that unless they are endorsed under conditions of liberty, they cannot properly guide a flourishing life. Furthermore, in the vast majority of cases, people will find it crucial to pursue their ideals in concert with others. Therefore, protecting the ability of people to live in accordance with their ideals also requires protecting their ability to form peaceful associations with others and to communicate freely with them. Of course there may be social costs to such protections, and as the costs increase, some limitations may be acceptable. But all societies must provide a certain minimal standard of protection for liberty of conscience.

Moving on to the issue of essential resources, James Nickel argues that "One of the most important ways in which the list of human rights in the Universal Declaration of Human Rights differs from earlier lists is that it includes rights to economic benefits and services" (Nickel 1987: 147). This is an important point, but Nickel seems excessively optimistic when he continues: "The idea that all people have rights to provision for their physical needs has received widespread acceptance in this [twentieth] century." In fact, there remains considerable controversy about whether a right even to subsistence-level resources should be recognized as a basic human right. We will discuss some of these objections in chapter 5. For now, I want simply to emphasize that no one could seriously doubt that without access to a minimally adequate share of resources, there can be little hope of living a satisfactory life. Furthermore, the provision of resources at a level higher than bare biological subsistence is necessary in order to secure other rights, such as the right to political participation and to a basic education. Therefore, when I refer to the provision of a minimally adequate share of resources, I mean providing not only those resources that are necessary for biological survival, but also the resources required in order to be able meaningfully to exercise the other basic rights.

The point to be emphasized, once again, is that this access must be *secure*. There is, in fact, a reciprocal relationship between political rights and the right to an adequate share of resources. As we have seen, without adequate resources, a right to participation is empty and cannot provide a check on the power of political authorities. But equally, without a right to political participation, access to necessary resources is not secure. As Shue emphasizes:

> It is not possible to enjoy full rights to security or to subsistence without also having rights to participate effectively in the control of security and subsistence. A right is the basis for a certain kind of demand: a demand the fulfillment of which ought to be socially guaranteed. Without channels through which the demand can be made known to those who ought to be guaranteeing its fulfillment, when it is in fact being ignored, one cannot exercise the right. (Shue 1986: 76–7)

What is missing in the case of the benevolent dictator who provides his subjects with physical security and basic resources is a social guarantee. And in the absence of a social guarantee, the individual remains vulnerable to other forms of abuse: "People who lack protection against violations of their physical security can, if they are free, fight back against their attackers or flee, but people who lack essentials, such as food, because of forces beyond their control, often can do nothing and are on their own utterly helpless" (Shue 1986: 25). Just as rights to security, basic liberty of conscience, and access to necessary resources are insecure without a right to political participation, they are also insecure without a right to personal property. An individual with no property rights is dependent on the largess of others and is therefore subject to domination at their hands, even if he is getting enough to eat at the moment. I should note that this argument generates only limited basic rights to personal property. In particular, it does not establish a basic right to ownership of the means of production or, for that matter, a right to participate in collective decisions concerning how the means of production are to be used. Nor does it generate an argument for any particular economic regime or scheme of taxation.

Finally, a right to basic education rules out the more extreme cases such as attempts fully to isolate a society from all external influences or to prevent women from receiving a basic education. However, as with other basic rights, the precise form and extent of this requirement will depend in part on the social environment and available resources. Like most of the other rights, it is valuable both for its own sake and for its support for the other basic rights. Unless a person has the tools necessary for a basic understanding of how the world works – both the natural and the social world – she has little chance of living a satisfactory life. Similarly, when this right is violated – when individuals are kept illiterate and ignorant – they are unable to secure their other rights, and are vulnerable to the capricious decisions of others. Once again, we see that when we adopt an institutional focus, there are many reciprocal relationships among the basic human rights.

5
Challenges to Human Rights

The list of human rights that I provided in chapter 4 can be challenged from either of two directions. It might be said that it is too limited and exclusive, or too extensive and inclusive. First, some might ask why other goods should not be protected in the same way as those that I have listed. Three proposed additional rights call for greater discussion: first, a right to *democratic* political institutions (and not merely a right to political participation); second, a right to an egalitarian distribution of resources (and not only to a minimal, threshold share); third, a right to cultural protection (beyond the worst forms of persecution that are prohibited by liberty of conscience). We will discuss the issues which each of these challenges raises below – democracy in chapter 6; economic distribution in chapter 7; and culture in chapter 8. But in this chapter I want to focus on the opposite challenge – either that the list I have given is too broad and affords protection to interests that are not universally important, or that there are no human rights at all.

The most radical challenge to human rights simply denies that they exist at all. There is a long history of such challenges (Waldron 1987), but here we will only consider one well-known argument, a clear version of which is presented by Alasdair MacIntyre. He asserts that it is "plain" that

> there are no such rights, and belief in them is one with belief in witches and in unicorns.

> The best reason for asserting so bluntly that there are no such rights is indeed of precisely the same type as the best reason which we possess for asserting that there are no witches and the best reason which we possess for asserting that there are no unicorns: every attempt to give good reasons for believing that there *are* such rights has failed. (MacIntyre 1984: 69)

It is, of course, a matter of dispute how strong the best arguments for basic human rights are, but MacIntyre's dogmatic dismissal is misguided. A human right is a very different kind of thing from a witch or a unicorn. Those creatures purport to be physical objects, and therefore subject to explanation in terms of natural science, while a human right indicates a norm or standard or ideal. In fact, MacIntyre doesn't seem to have the argument against witches and unicorns quite right. The reason we don't believe in witches and unicorns is not only that arguments *for* their existence have failed. It's that arguments *against* their existence are strong. Our best understanding of how the world works is *incompatible* with the existence of witches and unicorns. Their purported magical powers are in conflict with the account of the world provided by science. In contrast, claims about human rights do not conflict with scientific claims any more than other moral claims do. As we have seen, it is a mistake to attribute to them any kind of special metaphysical status.

A more moderate challenge accepts the existence of some human rights, such as a right to physical security and to certain political rights, but rejects so-called social and economic rights. The philosopher Maurice Cranston, for example, criticizes what he calls the "slovenly and muddled way of thinking" that led to the recognition not only of political rights but also of economic and social rights in the Universal Declaration of Human Rights (Cranston 1962: 35). The problem, Cranston argues, is that the " 'political rights' can be readily secured by legislation. The economic and social rights can rarely, if ever, be secured by legislation alone" (p. 37). Furthermore, he argues, "For a government to provide social security, it needs to do more than make laws; it needs to have access to very great wealth; and most governments in the world today are poor and cannot raise money" (p. 38). Because the material resources that would be necessary to satisfy (purported) economic rights are not available in poor countries, they fail the test of "practicability" (p. 36), and are, therefore, no rights at all. "At best," Cranston explains, economic rights are "hypothetical right[s], something they should have if they could have it" (p. 37).

In reply, notice first of all that Cranston seems to be assuming that simply making laws is sufficient to protect political rights, but that material resources are required in order to satisfy (purported) economic and social rights. This contrast is at the very least exaggerated, since no law can secure any basic human right unless adequate resources are devoted to enforcing it. Second, it is important not to demean the importance of what he calls "hypothetical rights." Although it may be true that under current social conditions, certain basic rights cannot adequately be protected, this should be grounds not for disparaging those rights, but rather for recognizing the importance of changing the social conditions. However, the most serious problem with Cranston's argument is that he focuses exclusively on whether an individual country is able to provide sufficient protection for its population. There is, however, no reason to assume that basic rights generate duties only among people who share a country. A basic right not to be tortured generates duties on all people of the world not to torture anyone and to assist in the creation of institutions everywhere that prevent torture (although, as we have seen, these duties may be of different weights). Similarly, a basic right to essential resources generates a duty on all people to assist in setting up institutions that secure them for all people (although, again, these duties may be of different weights). In the 1960s and 1970s it was sometimes argued that it was physically impossible to feed all of the people of the world (Hardin 1996). Few people make that argument today, for the good reason that it simply is not true. Unfortunately, it remains the case that some countries are not able to satisfy the basic needs of their own populations. The proper conclusion is not that in poor countries there is no basic human right to essential resources, but rather that sometimes this right can be secured only with the assistance of foreigners. As a variation on this argument, it is sometimes said that the financial burdens on wealthy countries, if they were to recognize the duties generated by a basic human right to subsistence, would be overwhelming. We will look at such arguments in chapter

7 in some detail, but it appears that Henry Shue is right when he says that such arguments are typically "laughable nonsense" (Shue 1996: 104).

At times, however, Cranston hints at a more general argument that depends not on the undefended assumption that the duties generated by basic human rights are limited by borders. This alternative argument is suggested by his claim that basic human rights are "for the most part rights against government interference with a man's activities" (Cranston 1962: 37).[1] This thought is sometimes presented in terms of skepticism about so-called positive rights, which involve not only protection *against* something (such as torture or murder) but a right *to* something (such as food or potable water) (Bedau 1979: 36–9). Notice that this contrast is not the same as the contrast between negative and positive *duties* discussed in chapter 4. One might think that there is a tight correspondence between negative rights and negative duties and between positive rights and positive duties, but this is a mistake. Physical security is sometimes thought to be the clearest example of a negative right. However, respecting it generates both negative and positive duties. To be sure, it generates a negative duty on government officials not to authorize or engage in torture or rape as part of their official duties. But securing this right certainly requires more. The government must take active, positive steps to protect people from torture and rape. Furthermore, contrary to Cranston's suggestion, these steps may be costly, and citizens will have a positive duty to pay their fair share (through taxes) in order for the government to be able to provide these protections (Buchanan 2004: 184, 196; Holmes and Sunstein 1999). Shue is convincing when he argues that "the common notion that *rights* can be divided into rights to forbearance (so-called negative rights), as if some rights have correlative duties only to avoid depriving, and rights to aid (so-called positive rights), as if some rights have correlative duties only to aid, is thoroughly misguided. . . . It is duties, not rights, that can be divided among avoidance and aid, and protection" (Shue 1996: 53). Skepticism about the existence of positive *rights* is largely based on a confusion. I should note, finally, that as Buchanan points out, all of this is "consistent with the view, held by some moral theorists, that so-called negative duties (duties not to kill, harm, etc.) are 'stricter' or weightier than so-called positive duties. However, it is one thing to say that negative duties (sometimes) have some sort of priority over positive ones, but quite another that we have no positive duties regarding persons" (Buchanan 2004: 91).

As we saw in chapter 3, the duties and strategies of foreigners must be sensitive to the nature of the threat to different basic rights. While it is true that food and other resources are sometimes intentionally destroyed or withheld as part of a deliberate strategy, the more typical threat to secure access to necessary resources is poverty. Of course, the causes of poverty are often complicated and controversial. But the typical case in which necessary resources are insecure differs greatly from a case in which, say, members of an ethnic minority are systematically terrorized by government officials. This is not because of any metaphysical difference between two types of rights, but due to the nature of the typical threats to each. While it may make sense for foreigners to attempt to pressure government officials to stop them from engaging in systematic torture, assistance may be what is required when a society is unable to provide necessary resources. Of course, when the withholding of food is used as a weapon of war, the case becomes more like the former. This shows that it is not some fundamental difference in the nature of the rights that is at issue, but rather the kind of threat to their security, and the strategies will be most effective in addressing those deprivations.

Many other critics, while not rejecting human rights outright, have challenged their universality and claimed that they are culturally biased. This is frequently presented in terms of the claim that so-called Asian values are incompatible with Western conceptions of human rights. We will use the debate about Asian values and human rights as a case study of the charge that human rights are objectionably biased and culturally specific. However, I should stress that this charge is made not only by defenders of Asian values. As we will see below, despite the fact that the creators of the Universal Declaration of Human Rights were a truly cosmopolitan group and in no way exclusively Western, some critics charge that human rights are "fundamentally Eurocentric" (Mutua 2002: 11) or "A Western Construct with Limited Applicability" (Pollis and Schwab 1979). In the broadest terms, we can organize our thinking about this debate in terms of three possible positions. The first holds that traditional Asian values are, in fact, compatible with universal human rights. The second asserts that traditional Asian values are incompatible with human rights, and that this shows that the purportedly universal human rights are appropriately applied (at most) only to certain Western societies. A third position agrees that traditional Asian values are incompatible with universal human rights, but maintains that this shows the need to reform or abandon those traditional values.

As we have seen, it is important that our account of human rights be tolerant of cultural diversity and legitimate social differences. In particular, we want the justification of human rights to be compatible with many conflicting yet reasonable comprehensive religions and ethical doctrines. On the other hand, it would be a mistake to attempt to identify basic human rights by taking an empirical survey of the values that different societies happen to share (J. Cohen 2004: 200). For example, it may be that all societies have a norm against slavery. However, our reason for including a prohibition against slavery as a basic human right is not that all societies happen to have such a norm. If a society were gradually to loosen its prohibition of slavery, we would *not* be tempted to revise our account of human rights in order to accommodate that society. Instead, we would properly condemn that society's practice. Neither the location of the origin of the ideas nor the extent of current violations *by themselves* refute the universality of basic human rights (Donnelly 1999: 69; Nussbaum 2004: 153). Still, if it turned out that a significant portion of the world rejected what we have identified as basic human rights, this would provide us with a good reason for examining the situation more closely. Perhaps we might conclude that we improperly excluded an unfamiliar way of organizing society that, on reflection, we can see could enable and promote good and valuable lives.

One difficulty with the "Asian values" critique of human rights is definitional: defenders must identify the specific values that are supposed to be incompatible with universal human rights. As Amartya Sen points out, "The temptation to see Asia as one unit reveals, in fact, a distinctly Eurocentric perspective" (Sen 1997: 13). He goes on to observe that

"In practice, the advocates of 'Asian values' have tended to look primarily at East Asia as the region of particular applicability." There remains a problem, however, since "East Asia itself has much diversity, and there are many variations between Japan and China and Korea and other parts of East Asia" (pp. 13–14). Even if we focus on a single society or tradition, we can find widely different interpretations of the relevant practices and texts. As the Singaporean diplomat Bilahari Kausikan points out, "Most Asian societies have such long histories and rich cultures that it is possible to 'prove' nearly anything about them if the context of the recovered references is ignored" (Kausikan 1997: 30). It should come as no surprise that in any tradition, including Western traditions, practices and texts can be found that are incompatible with our modern understanding of human rights. By themselves, such practices and texts don't show that the tradition is incompatible with human rights unless one can also show that they are central or essential elements of that tradition.

Instead of entering into debates about which interpretation of a tradition or value system is more authentic, we will turn to the substantive claims that critics make when challenging the universality of human rights. There are three main arguments to consider. First, it is sometimes said that human rights hinder economic development, and that societies may legitimately choose development over human rights; second, many critics claim that human rights are excessively individualistic; third, some argue that recognizing universal human rights does not leave sufficient room for diversity and leads to an imperial foreign policy. On the first issue, it is sometimes said that human rights must be sacrificed, at least temporarily, in the interest of economic development. As the former Prime Minister of Singapore, Lee Kuan Yew, has stated, "As prime minister of Singapore, my first task was to lift my country out of the degradation that poverty, ignorance and disease had wrought. Since it was dire poverty that made for such a low priority given to human life, all other things became secondary" (quoted in Bell 1996: 643).

I have included a right to essential resources as a basic human right, and therefore in this framework Lee can be understood as giving priority to one set of rights over others. It is possible for rights to conflict with one another; however, our best evidence is that there is no fundamental conflict between economic rights and civil and political rights. In general, this is a trade-off that does not have to be made. Amartya Sen points out that there is little evidence that respect for basic human rights interferes with economic development:

> Systematic empirical studies give no real support to the claim that there is a conflict between political rights and economic performance. The directional linkage seems to depend on many other circumstances, and while some statistical investigations note a weakly negative relations, others find a strongly positive one. On balance, the hypothesis that there is no relation between the two in either direction is hard to reject. (Sen 1997: 11; cf. Przeworski and Limongi 1993)

A recent study by Morton Halperin, Joseph Siegle, and Michael Weinstein makes a somewhat stronger claim. They argue that "low-income democracies and democratizing countries have outperformed their authoritarian counterparts on a full range of development indicators. . . . [W]hen one looks at the experience of developing countries as a whole, those with more representative and pluralistic political systems have typically developed significantly more rapidly, broadly, and consistently than those with closed systems" (Halperin et al. 2005: 10–11). These authors are careful to point out that they aim only to establish that democracy and development are compatible with one another, not that one inevitably leads to the other (pp. 29–30). Still, their results are striking in countering a common view about the economic superiority of authoritarian states.

Although there seems to be little direct relationship between human rights and economic development in general, there is evidence that democratic institutions help prevent economic catastrophes (Halperin et al. 2005: 33). Sen has famously argued that

> no famine has ever taken place in the history of the world in a functioning democracy – be it economically rich (as in contemporary Western Europe or North America) or relatively poor (as in postindependence India, or Botswana, or Zimbabwe). Famines have tended to occur in colonial territories governed by rulers from elsewhere (as in British India or in

an Ireland administered by alienated English rulers), or in one-party states (as in the Ukraine in the 1930s, or China during 1958–1961, or Cambodia in the 1970s), or in military dictatorships (as in Ethiopia, or Somalia, or some of the Sahel countries in the near past). (Sen 1999: 16; cf. Sen 1981)

On balance, then, the argument that political and civil rights must be sacrificed for economic development lacks empirical support. Furthermore, even if there were a necessary trade-off, this would not challenge the universality of human rights. The most that we would be able to conclude is that we must resolve conflicts among basic human rights, not that they should be rejected altogether.

The second argument against basic human rights asserts that they are in some way excessively individualistic or that they emphasize individual liberty at the expense of responsibility or communal values that are (supposedly) characteristic of East Asian societies. Kausikan argues this way when he claims that "many East and Southeast Asians tend to look askance at the starkly individualistic ethos of the West in which authority tends to be seen as oppressive and rights are an individual's 'trump' over the state" (Kausikan 1993: 36; cf. Donnelly 1999: 78). Lee Kuan Yew, in addition to claiming that human rights hinder economic development, also makes this kind of anti-individualistic argument:

> The fundamental difference between Western concepts of society and government and East Asian concepts . . . is that Eastern societies believe that the individual exists in the context of his family. He is not pristine and separate. The family is part of the extended family, and then friends and the wider society. The ruler or the government does not try to provide for a person what the family best provides. (Zakaria 1994: 113)

Together with the economic argument, it is on the basis of this "communitarian" understanding of the self that Lee justifies "interfering in the private lives of citizens. . . . – who your neighbor is, how you live, the noise you make, how you spit, or what language you use. We decide what's right. Never mind what the people think" (quoted in Englehart 2000: 554).

It is a significant distortion to characterize this position as being *simply* anti-individualistic. In fact, in addition to being anti-individualistic, it is equally opposed to communities and groups – from families to civil associations to religious institutions – with the single exception of the state itself. In this context, Lee's praise of the family and friends is empty rhetoric. When a government violates basic human rights, it not only restricts individual liberty. It also usurps authority from families and all other associations, giving itself unlimited and arbitrary power. Allen Buchanan makes the point bluntly:

> Since the end of the religious wars of the sixteenth and seventeenth century in Europe, and with greater effectiveness today because they are supported by international legal institutions, rights to freedom of expression and association and to freedom of religion have played a valuable role in protecting *communities*. Therefore, to maintain that these core human rights are only rights for atomistic individuals requires something approaching willful stupidity. They are rights that contribute greatly to the flourishing of communities, whether they are religious, political, or "lifestyle" communities. (Buchanan 2004: 156)

Although policies restricting individual liberty often present themselves as communitarian, in fact they leave room only for an authoritarian political structure. This is hardly a formula for strengthening community identification and loosening the grip of a narrow self-interested atomism, since the use of force will inevitably be viewed as an external imposition. On the contrary, it is only when basic human rights are respected that individuals are able freely to develop deep, lasting, and morally admirable identification with their communities.

Putting aside the dubious argument that respecting human rights impedes economic development, and the mistaken assumption that they somehow weaken communities, we are left with one final consideration. Time and time again, defenders of the Asian values argument criticize Western governments and non-governmental organizations (NGOs) for promoting abstract human rights without adequate sensitivity to the cultural and social context in which they are to be applied.[2] When this argument is made, it is typically conceded that there are a few human rights that are truly universal. Critics like Kausikan concede that "The West has a legitimate right and moral duty to promote those core human rights, even if it is tempered by limited influence." (Kausikan 1993: 39–40). Nonetheless, he claims "The Western media, NGOs, and human rights activists, especially in the United States, tend to press the human rights dialogue beyond the legitimate insistence on humane standards of behavior by calling for the summary implementation of abstract concepts without regard for a country's unique cultural, social, economic, and political circumstances" (Kausikan 1993: 33). Similarly, Daniel A. Bell acknowledges a core set of universal human rights, but objects that "The most influential Anglo-American political philosophers today still seem compelled by a tradition of universalist moral reasoning that proposes one final solution to the question of the ideal polity yet paradoxically draws only on the moral aspirations and political practices found in Western societies" (Bell 2000: 6). The useful reminder in all of this is simply that there is not just one institutional arrangement that can be designed effectively to protect core human rights. Local cultural values and history are certainly relevant to determining the most effective strategy to ensure that core human rights are not violated. Bell is correct when he argues: "If the ultimate aim of human rights diplomacy is to persuade others of the value of human rights, it is more likely that the struggle to promote human rights can be won if it is fought in ways that build on, rather than challenge, local cultural traditions" (Bell 1996: 651).

However, despite Bell's suggestion to the contrary, most theorists of human rights recognize this. As Jack Donnelly, who is singled out by Bell for criticism, stresses, "internationally recognized human rights leave considerable space for distinctively Asian implementations of these rights." He continues that, according to the approach he advocates, "Human rights are treated as essentially universal, but substantial space is allowed for variations in implementing these universal norms" (Donnelly 1999: 83). For example, there are many different institutional mechanisms that could be used to ensure that everyone receives necessary resources, and societies should be free to select whichever one they believe to be most consistent with their other commitments and values. It is also inaccurate to paint NGOs with such a broad brush and declare that they are generally insensitive to local concerns. As Michael Freeman observes, "NGOs provide an important bridge between the remote world of law, politics and bureaucracy, on the one hand, and the actual experience of human-rights violations, on the other. . . . Ironically, governments that complain of the Western bias of NGOs often prevent the formation of NGOs in their own countries" (Freeman 2002: 146).

It is impossible not to notice that many of the defenders of the "Asian values" critique of human rights are themselves government officials, who are able to maintain their power precisely by denying the basic political rights that would allow political opponents to criticize and challenge their rule. The temptation is strong to agree with Kenneth Christie that the claim that Asian values are incompatible with human rights often "serve[s] as a device for authoritarian regimes in the region to enhance their own, often declining, legitimacy, and protect the security of their particular regime" (Christie 1995: 204). This was clearly the case, for example, when General Than Shwe, the ruler of Myanmar (Burma) and a notorious violator of human rights, argued that "The external forces that bear malice towards us are inciting the people by using human rights and democracy as an excuse. The Western countries' human rights and standards of democracy cannot be the same as our Asian standards" (quoted in Christie 1995: 205). But it is also true of "soft-authoritarian" societies like Singapore, where the ruling government regularly arrests and holds political opponents without trial (Englehart 2000: 549). Indeed, Donald Emmerson points out that Singapore's authorities have often arrested those who criticize, even obliquely, their official "Asian values" argument (Emmerson 1995). As even Bell concedes, "it was easy to dismiss – rightly so, in most cases – the Asian challenge as nothing but a self-serving play by government leaders to justify their authoritarian rule in the face of increasing demands for democracy at home and abroad" (Bell 2000: 8).

Still, it is not only powerful politicians who try to defend Asian values against what they view as the imperialism of Western human rights (Bell 2000: 9–10). One reads over and over again about the failures of the West and its "missionary zeal to whop the heathen along the path of righteousness and remake the world in its own image" (Kausikan 1993: 33). Although it is certainly appropriate to criticize many aspects of US and Western foreign policy, the most compelling of these criticisms are based precisely on the *failure* of Western countries to respect basic human rights. These condemnations, therefore, inadvertently reveal something else: namely, a deep psychological defensiveness concerning foreign criticisms of one's own society. Such a reaction is very common, and certainly not characteristic of Asian societies alone. This visceral resistance to foreign criticism should not lead us to abandon our commitment to the universality of core human rights. However, it should serve as a caution concerning the limitations of what foreigners can accomplish and how their criticisms should be presented even when correct. At its best, foreign criticism can serve as a much-needed opportunity and spur to reflect on alternatives and to open paths for possible change. At its worst, it can trigger a self-protective, nationalistic backlash that serves only to tarnish domestic advocates of human rights with the charge of foreign collusion. Again, none of this undermines the universality of basic human rights, but it does raise important pragmatic considerations concerning the best course of action when human rights are violated in other countries.

One final objection to the idea of human rights takes its inspiration from the account of realism in foreign policy discussed in chapter 3. The idea is perhaps less an argument than simply an expression of pessimism with respect to the power of moral ideals generally. Human rights are said to be too utopian, since they are regularly flouted throughout the world, and the majority of people in the world today live without secure provision of their vital needs. After all, human rights do not enforce themselves, and there is no international mechanism powerful enough to prevent their violation. When one looks back over the horrors of the twentieth century[3] and the extent of severe poverty in the world today (see chapter 7), it is hard not to feel despair.

I will respond to this criticism by briefly recounting the creation of, and some of the influence of, the Universal Declaration of Human Rights. It is important to remember that the widespread recognition of basic human rights is a very recent development. While principles of toleration and limits on state powers are very old and are found in many different traditions, the idea that all people have rights in virtue of their humanity that all others (and not only members of their own group) must respect is quite recent. And the idea that these rights should be codified in international law, to put limits on the legitimate use of power not only among societies but *within* a society is even more recent. Well into the twentieth century, human rights were thought to have essentially no role in international relations. The 1919 Covenant that established the League of Nations (part of the Treaty of Versailles that ended World War I), for example, made no mention of human rights. According to the dominant understanding of international relations at the time, it was assumed that no country was properly concerned with the internal affairs of others. This idea of strong state sovereignty is sometimes known as "Westphalian sovereignty," although the political scientist Stephen Krasner argues that "It was not clearly articulated until the end of the eighteenth century" (Krasner 1999: 20). As we saw in chapter 2, the norm of non-intervention while often violated in practice, at least as an ideal, granted to each state an important measure of self-determination. The problem was that in addition to ruling out foreign intervention, it also ruled out any concern on the part of foreigners for domestic violations of human rights.

This Wesphalian understanding of international relations was still evident in the Charter of the UN, adopted in 1945. It is perhaps most clear in Article 2, paragraph 7, which states that "Nothing contained in the present Charter shall authorize the United Nations to intervene in matters which are essentially within the domestic jurisdiction of any state" (United Nations 1945).[4] In fact, according to Mary Ann Glendon:

> The promotion of fundamental rights and freedoms was far from central to the thinking of any of the Big Three [USA, Britain, and the Soviet Union] as they debated the shape and purpose of the United Nations. This was not surprising: it was not self-evident that the proposed international organization ought to be concerned with such matters. For one thing, international lawyers regarded a state's treatment of its own citizens, with rare exceptions, as that nation's own business.
>
> That began to change, however, in the waning days of the war, as appalling details of the Nazi reign of terror were coming to light and the Allies faced the question of how to deal with major war criminals. (Glendon 2001: 9; cf. Morsink 1999: ch. 2)

The creation of the Nuremberg Principles, the trials of Nazi and Japanese war criminals, and the passage of the Convention on the Prevention and Punishment of the Crime of Genocide in 1948, all represent the erosion of the traditional strong notion of state sovereignty. Of particular significance was the requirement in Article 1 of the Convention on Genocide that the contracting parties "undertake to prevent and punish" genocide "whether committed in time of peace or in time of war" (United Nations 1948a).[5] In addition, several references to human rights were included in the UN Charter. For example, the preface states that "people of the united nations [are] determined to . . . reaffirm faith in fundamental human rights, in the dignity and worth of the human person, in the equal rights of men and women and of nations large and small" (cf. Freeman 2002: 33). But in terms of shaping world opinion in support of basic human rights, the most important act was the creation of what one recent commentator has called "the most important legal document in the history of the world" (Drinan 2001: 9), the Universal Declaration of Human Rights.

The UN Charter set up only one special commission: the Human Rights Commission. It was to include permanent representatives from the USA, the Soviet Union, the UK, France, China, and thirteen rotating seats. The Commission was charged with generating a Universal Declaration of Human Rights to submit to the General Assembly. With (the recently widowed) Eleanor Roosevelt as chair, Peng-chun Change, "a Chinese Renaissance man . . . devoted to traditional Chinese music and literature but conversant with Islamic and Western culture as well," as vice-chair, and Charles Malik, a Lebanese philosophy professor as secretary, the leadership of the Commission "symbolically repres-ent[ed] West, East, and, in the case of Malik, a crossroads of many cultures" (Glendon 2001: 33). In creating the UDHR, the Commission was assisted by a Committee on the Theoretical Bases of Human Rights, formed by the UN's Educational, Scientific and Cultural Organization (UNESCO). This committee solicited input from experts and statesmen from around the world concerning their ideas for a universal declaration of human rights. According to Glendon, the results indicated that the principles underlying the draft Declaration were present in many cultural and religious traditions, though not always expressed in terms of rights. Somewhat to the UNESCO group's surprise, the list of basic rights and values submitted by their far-flung correspondents were broadly similar. UNESCO's list of widely shared norms included both political and civil liberties and social and economic rights. (Glendon 2001: 76)

After a year and a half of sometimes acrimonious meetings, the Human Rights Commission presented the UDHR to the General Assembly, which voted to accept it on December 10, 1948 (one day after accepting the Convention on Genocide), with 48 countries voting in favor, eight abstaining, and none voting against.

The UDHR did not include any mechanism of enforcement. The Human Rights Commission had set up three drafting committees to work in parallel: one on the Declaration, which would state principles and ideals; one on a Covenant, which would be a legally binding statement of international law; and one on implementation mechanisms (Glendon 2001: 86). However, it soon became clear that "*all* of the major powers were fiercely protective of their sovereignty, and Britain of its colonial empire" (Glendon 2001: 87). The more powerful countries, principally the USA, the UK, and the Soviet Union, simply would not submit to binding international constraints. In the case of the USA, opposition to any legally binding human rights covenant was made explicit by Secretary of State John Foster Dulles in 1953 (Glendon 2001: 205). The resulting UDHR, therefore, was presented as an inspiring ideal, but not as legally binding and without any mechanism of enforcement. Still, Eleanor Roosevelt "believed wholeheartedly that a declaration, though not legally binding, would be much more than a vague proclamation. Like the American Declaration of Independence, it would announce the goals toward which all nations would commit themselves to strive" (Glendon 2001: 86). In retrospect, as Johannes Morsink points out, the lack of enforcement mechanisms "may have been a blessing in disguise. Because it floats above all local and regional contingencies and is a statement of more or less abstract moral rights and principles, the Declaration served as midwife in the birth of . . . other more concrete and detailed international instruments" (Morsink 1999: p. xi; cf. 19–20). For example, "it has been estimated that the Declaration has inspired or served as a model for the rights provisions of some ninety constitutions" (Glendon 2001: 228; Morsink 1999: p. ix). In addition, there are now hundreds of NGOs, such as Human Rights Watch and Amnesty International, with millions of members devoted to monitoring compliance with, and publicizing violations of, basic human rights. There is little doubt that Morsink is right when he claims that "the Universal Declaration of Human Rights is the moral anchor of this worldwide movement" (Morsink 1999: p. xii).

As the Cold War heated up, the USA and the USSR came to view the UDHR largely as a tool with which to attempt to score propaganda points against each other. As Glendon explains,

> All through the cold war, the United States and the USSR traded charges of human rights violations while overlooking their own failures and those of their client states. The Soviet Union used the Declaration's antidiscrimination articles and its social and economic provisions to berate the United States and its friends, while the Western bloc badgered the Communist countries for failing to protect free expression and free elections. A wedge was driven through the heart of the Declaration, severing its firm link between freedom and solidarity. Thus began the now prevalent pick-and-choose approach to interpreting its thirty integrated articles. (Glendon 2001: 214)

In 1951, while work proceeded on the implementing Covenant that would turn the UDHR into binding international law, the UN bowed to these political pressures and divided it in two: one to cover political and civil liberties and the other devoted to economic, social, and cultural rights. Glendon argues:

> In practical terms the move made sense, but separating the political/civil liberties from the social/economic rights had a heavy cost: it undercut the Declaration's message that one set of values could not long endure without the other. It suggested a retreat from the proposition that a better standard of living cannot be accomplished without larger freedom, and that

freedom is threatened by dehumanizing living conditions. (Glendon 2001: 202)

The two Covenants were finally approved by the General Assembly in 1966, and went into effect in 1976. Together with the UDHR, the International Covenant on Economic, Social, and Cultural Rights and the International Covenant on Civil and Political Rights are known collectively as the "International Bill of Rights." By 1999, 141 states had become parties to the Covenant on Civil and Political Rights, and 144 were parties to the International Covenant on Economic, Social, and Cultural Rights.[6]

At the conclusion of the Cold War, many people hoped that a new era of respect for human rights could emerge. One result was the UN Conference on Human Rights, held in Vienna in 1993. Although some delegates initially made an "Asian values" argument against human rights, eventually representatives of all 171 countries that were present re-affirmed "their commitment to the purposes and principles contained in the Charter of the United Nations and the Universal Declaration of Human Rights" and pledged to "fulfil their obligations to promote universal respect for, and observance and protection of, all human rights and funda-mental freedoms for all." "The universal nature of these rights and freedoms," it continued, "is beyond question" (United Nations 1993).[7] Today, no country in the world is willing to say openly that it violates basic human rights or that it rules in anything but the interest of its citizens. When viewed in his-torical perspective, the current nearly unanimous consensus concerning this moral ideal is truly astonishing. Of course, saying that one affirms an ideal is quite different from achiev-ing it, or even taking credible steps toward implementing it. No doubt many affirmations of principle are hypocritical. It is certainly true that words alone cannot protect basic human rights. Nonetheless, words can be significant.

The cynicism and resignation characteristic of those who say that affirmations of human rights cannot be effective is unwarranted. It is easy to misunderstand the level and manner in which moral principles and ideals operate. Their effects are sometimes indirect and may take time to become visible. Moral principles cannot stop the violation of human rights directly, but they can shape the social environment that gives rise to violations. Governments often take an important step when they explicitly affirm their support for basic human rights, even if they have no intention of living up to those ideals (Risse and Sikkink 1999). When a violator of human rights is forced to affirm allegiance to principles of human rights, this often serves as an important boost for domestic opposition and NGOs. For example, despite their initial reluctance to include any discussion of human rights on the agenda, the USSR relented and included them on the agenda at the Conference on Security and Cooperation in Europe that began in 1972. The eventual result was the Helsinki Final Act, signed in 1975, which affirmed specific rights and made reference to the UDHR. According to the political scientist Daniel Thomas, the "East Bloc leadership accepted [the inclusion of human rights] in hopes of gaining economic resources and political legitimacy" (Thomas 1999: 208). And although the Communist regimes attempted to portray the accords as "a ratification of the status quo," activists from Czechoslovakia to Poland to Russia saw it as "a promising and unprecedented opportunity to challenge the repressiveness of those regimes. Whatever the Communist authorities had intended by the signature on the Final Act, these activists would invoke their official commitments to human rights as if they had been sincere" (p. 209). Among other things, this led to the formation of the Charter 77 movement in Czechoslovakia and, perhaps more indirectly, to the recognition of the Solidarity trade union in Poland in 1980. While it is true that "The ultimate linchpin of real political change in Eastern Europe . . . was the accession of a reform-minded leadership in Moscow," there can be little doubt that "the emergence and persistence of human rights movements across the Soviet Union and Eastern Europe after Helsinki, culminating in the spectacular rise of Solidarity, had already delegitimated Communist rule in popular eyes, and forced elites across the bloc to question how long the status quo could be maintained" (pp. 228–9; cf. Donnelly 1998: 81). Despite the fact that official acceptance of them was largely insincere, they took on a life of their own in ways that were almost entirely unanticipated by those who dismissed them as "only words" (cf. Thomas 2001).

6
Political Legitimacy

With this account of human rights in place, we can now consider the role that they should play in global justice. It is easy enough to conclude that when we look at domestic institutions, justice demands that *at a minimum* they should be designed to protect basic human rights. The more difficult questions concern the duties of foreigners when domestic institutions fail to protect or actively violate basic human rights. But to begin, I want to approach these questions from the opposite direction and ask what are the consequences for global justice when a social structure *does* adequately protect the basic human rights of its citizens. My account will be based on an interpretation of John Rawls's *The Law of Peoples*.[1]

One of the more controversial elements of Rawls's *The Law of Peoples* concerns his discussion of what he calls "decent hierarchical societies."[2] These are societies that do not subscribe to liberal principles of justice. They may, for example, reject the democratic principle of "one person, one vote," or have an official state religion, or tolerate a significant degree of inequality in wealth. On the other hand, they do protect basic human rights (although, again, not the full array of rights protected in a liberal society) (Rawls 1999b: 65). In addition, they have a system of law adequate to "impose *bona fide* moral duties and obligations (distinct from human rights) on all persons within the people's territory" (pp. 65–6), and the law is administered openly and publicly with reference to "a common good idea of justice." In particular:

> Judges and other officials must be willing to address objections. They cannot refuse to listen, charging that the dissenters are incompetent and unable to understand, for then we would have not a decent consultation hierarchy, but a paternalistic regime. Moreover, should the judges and other officials listen, the dissenters are not required to accept the answer given to them; they may renew their protest, providing they explain why they are still dissatisfied, and their explanation in turn ought to receive a further and fuller reply. Dissent expresses a form of public protest and is permissible provided it stays within the basic framework of the common good idea of justice. (p. 72; cf. 61, 78)

These requirements represent significant moral demands that many actual societies fail to meet. As Rawls comments, "Laws supported merely by force are grounds for rebellion and resistance. They are routine in a slave society, but cannot belong to a decent one" (p. 88). So, on the one hand, a decent hierarchical society does meet certain minimal requirements – it is not what Rawls calls an "outlaw state." On the other hand, such a society does not even accept, let alone satisfy, the liberal principles of domestic justice that Rawls endorses: "To repeat, I am not saying that a decent hierarchical society is as reasonable and just as a liberal society" (p. 83).

The controversy concerns Rawls's claim that when a decent hierarchical society has a non-aggressive foreign policy, it should be fully tolerated by just liberal societies. (Such toleration is not due to outlaw states.) In other words, Rawls holds that the existence of a decent society would not violate his principles of global justice, even though it would violate his principles of domestic justice. Why should a society committed to liberal principles of justice tolerate certain kinds of injustice in a foreign society that it would not accept domestically? One possible answer emphasizes that even if one believes that the same principles of justice ought to apply to both domestic and foreign societies, the circumstances of application differ between the two. For example, there may be a greater likelihood of error in determining what justice requires in foreign countries than in one's own. Furthermore, efforts to

bring about changes in foreign countries may generate resentment and become counter-productive, or at a minimum have
harmful, though unintended, consequences. The ethos of a
society is crucial for the stability of just institutions, but this is
something that may be difficult to change, especially for outsiders. Following this line of thinking, Charles Beitz claims, "It
seems likely that the main objections to a general permission
to intervene in the cause of justice are practical rather than theoretical in the sense that they hold such intervention, in practice, to be difficult to calculate and control" (Beitz 1999: 83).
But Rawls is emphatic that the grounds for toleration are
deeper than such practical considerations:

> It is important to emphasize that the reasons for not imposing
> sanctions [on decent hierarchical societies] do not boil down
> solely to the prevention of possible error and miscalculation in
> dealing with a foreign people. The danger of error, miscalcu-
> lation, and also arrogance on the part of those who propose
> sanctions must, of course, be taken into account; yet decent
> hierarchical societies do have certain institutional features that
> deserve respect, even if their institutions as a whole are not suf-
> ficiently reasonable from the point of view of political liberal-
> ism or liberalism generally. (Rawls 1999b: 83–4)

For Rawls, toleration of decent hierarchical societies is not
merely a matter of instrumental concerns about the effectiveness of attempting to coerce a foreign country to become more
just. Why, then, does Rawls support the toleration of at least
certain kinds of injustice in the international realm? The
answer is not clear, and Rawls's critics have failed to find
any principled answer. Kok-Chor Tan, for example, claims
that Rawls's account is "blatantly inconsistent," since it "is
inspired more by the need to *accommodate* representatives of
[decent hierarchical societies], to ensure that his law of peoples
can be endorsed by some nonliberal states as well, than by the
goal of achieving stability for the right reasons" (Tan 2000:
30–1). And Thomas McCarthy asks rhetorically, "Why should
[a liberal, democratic people] surrender their basic *political*
principles for the sake of reaching agreement with peoples who
do not share them?" (McCarthy 1997: 209).
   I believe that a principled defense of Rawls's position is
possible. It depends on the concept of *legitimacy*, applied to

both law (more narrowly) and political orders (more generally).[3] The idea is that decent hierarchical societies have political institutions that meet a certain minimal threshold of legitimacy, and because of this, if they pursue a non-aggressive foreign policy, they are entitled to full toleration from other societies. To defend this position, two questions must be answered. First, why should toleration be based on legitimacy? And second, what are the standards for legitimacy?

At least since Aristotle, it has been widely recognized that a political order (a state) is necessary to achieve social justice. For some authors such as Hobbes, a commonwealth is required in order to escape from the war "of every man against every man" characteristic of the state of nature in which "nothing can be unjust. The notions of right and wrong, justice and injustice, have there no place" (Hobbes [1660] 1994: 76, 78; ch. 13, paras 8, 13). For Hobbes, the creation of a commonwealth establishes the conditions of justice in which the well-being of each individual is better secured. Kant rejects Hobbes's characterization of the state of nature. Yet he holds that outside a commonwealth there will inevitably be disagreement among individuals of good will concerning what justice requires. Political institutions are necessary for resolving such conflicts: "It is true that the state of nature need not, just because it is natural, be a state of *injustice*. . . . But it still would be a state *devoid of justice* . . . in which when rights are *in dispute* . . . there would be no judge competent to render a verdict having rightful force. Hence each may impel the other by force to leave this state and enter into a rightful condition [i.e. a commonwealth]" (Kant [1797] 1996: 90; §44 (Ak. vi. 312)). Even Nietzsche, who holds that justice properly understood involves "the battle *against* reactive feelings," asserts that the establishment of a modern state is the "most decisive" development in this cause. This is because only with a modern state can a society treat "infringements and arbitrary actions of individuals or entire groups as wanton acts against the law, as rebellion against the highest power itself, thereby diverting the feeling of its subjects away from the immediate injury caused by such wanton acts and thus achieving in the long run the opposite of what all revenge wants, which sees only the viewpoint of the injured one, allows only it to count" (Nietzsche [1887] 1998: 49–50; II, 11). These theorists understand justice in very different ways, and each has a different reason to believe that political institutions and law serve the cause of justice. Nonetheless, they all recognize, as does virtually every political philosopher with the exception of anarchists, that there is little hope achieving justice outside a political order.

Justice requires political structures that allow people to make collective, explicit, binding decisions. At least in modern, large-scale societies, this is done through institutions of law. As Habermas observes, "Modern states are characterized by the fact that political power is constituted in the form of positive law, which is to say enacted and coercive law" (Habermas 2002: 198). This does not mean that a society is responsible only for the laws that it enacts. Members of a society may be collectively responsible for social facts that they never explicitly sanctioned but that merely emerge unintended from their actions and omissions. Typically, however, if a society makes an explicit decision to address what it takes to be some problem, it will do so through changes in the law. It may, for example, directly prohibit or authorize certain kinds of conduct, or it may take other steps that aim to change patterns of behavior more indirectly. Furthermore, these decisions are typically made through *coercive* laws, since they are backed by at least an implicit threat of force.

Given the law's coercive nature, it is always possible to view it as imposing an external constraint on one's ability to act in accordance with one's preferences. But states claim that their laws are *legitimate* – that is, that they are justified. This means that individuals can view the law not simply as an external constraint on their freedom, but also as an expression of what they have reason to do as members of a political community. Habermas makes the point this way:

> Modern law leaves its addressees free to approach the law in either of two ways. They can consider norms merely as factual constraints on their freedom and take a strategic approach to the calculable consequences of possible rule violations, or they can comply with regulation "out of respect for the law." . . . It must at least be possible to obey laws not because they are compulsory but because they are legitimate. (Habermas 2002: 198–9)

What "respect for the law" requires is controversial. For some authors, including Rawls, there is a general duty to obey legitimate law (although it may be overridden by other moral considerations). Other authors deny that there is any such obligation. I remain agnostic on this question. The argument I make below depends on a weaker duty: namely, the duty not to interfere (by using force) with the institutions of legitimate law, including its creation and application (Edmundson 1998). This is part of the natural duty of justice, for justice requires that societies be able to make and carry out collective and binding decisions. Notice that this duty of noninterference holds for all individuals with respect to *all* legitimate systems of law, not only that of their own society.

We are now in a position to consider the criteria for legitimate law. In other words, under what conditions is the coercive imposition of the law justified, and when is there a duty not to interfere with its creation and application (and possibly a duty for citizens to obey)? One possible answer relies entirely on procedural elements. On this view, if a law is the outcome of a certain privileged procedure, say the majority vote of the citizens or of their duly elected representatives, then the law is legitimate. The problem with this is that it is too inclusive. Purely procedural requirements place no constraints on the content of law, and surely the content matters if we think that legitimate laws impose substantive moral duties on citizens. It would be unreasonable to demand of citizens that they not resist (or comply with) a law that enslaves them and deprives them of their basic rights, for example, simply because the majority votes for it. At the opposite extreme, we might consider the possibility that the only legitimate laws are the ones that are substantively fully just. On this view, there is no duty to resist a law unless it is just, regardless of its etiology. But this makes the standard for legitimacy too demanding. Certainly, political institutions should aim to produce laws that promote or are at least consistent with justice. (There may be other important goals, as well, such as reflecting the self-conception of the citizens.) But no political structure can guarantee that it will produce laws that are necessary for justice or even produce only those that are consistent with justice. Furthermore, as Kant stressed, we must expect that there will often be reasonable and sincere disagreement about what substantive justice requires in a society. To equate legitimacy with justice would undermine the ability of a society to make collective and binding decisions for itself. And, as we have seen, this capacity is something that is required by justice itself (even if this capacity will occasionally result in laws that are substantively unjust). The solution is to combine these two elements and to have both substantive and procedural components in our account of legitimacy. Substantively, laws must respect and protect basic human rights in order to be legitimate. But within this constraint there is broad discretion for a society to make its own collective binding decisions. A society does this by following the procedure specified by its constitution, which we may think of as the system of publicly recognized rules for making and applying (ordinary) laws.[4]

What procedural elements must a law satisfy in order to be legitimate? Remember, we are trying to find conditions that, when satisfied, allow us to say that a law reflects a collective decision of the society as a whole, even if not every person considered individually supports it. Specifically, is democracy required? The answer depends on how democracy is understood. In the most narrow sense, a political order is democratic only if it relies on majority rule based on the principle of one person, one vote. At the opposite extreme, we might call a society democratic whenever its laws can properly be said to represent the will of the people as whole, in which case the requirement of democracy won't impose any further conditions beyond what we already know legitimacy to require. The important point for us, however, is not how we define democracy, but whether legitimacy requires a particular institutional scheme. It seems that there are numerous institutional arrangements that can properly be said to produce collective decisions of the society, including, for example, in the USA with its electoral college and Senate;[5] Hegel's proposal, according to which individuals are represented through the "associations, communities, and corporations" of civil society of which they are members (Hegel [1821] 1991: sec. 308; cf. Rawls 1999b: 72–3); Mill's system of "plural voting" in which the more intelligent or better educated receive an extra vote (Mill [1861] 1991: 338; ch. 8, para. 12; cf. Thompson 1976: ch. 2; J. J. Miller 2003); and Iris Young's proposal for giving oppressed groups "veto power regarding specific policies that affect a group directly, such as reproductive rights policy for women, or land use policy for Indian reservations" (Young 1990: 184). Each of these arrangements rejects the principle of one person, one vote, and so none is democratic in the most narrow sense. On the other hand, if properly implemented and carried out as intended, decisions made by each of these structures could properly be described as collective decisions by the people of a society. Each could represent legitimate political order. This is not to say that they would be equally just. The crucial point is that legitimacy requires a workable mechanism through which individuals can publicly express their views concerning the common good, and that the society's political decisions reflect those public debates. Only then can the law properly be said to be a collective achievement of the society as a whole. This requirement is, of course, part of Rawls's account of decent societies, and I believe that it is the proper procedural requirement for legitimacy.[6]

So we can combine these ideas to say that a political structure and the laws that it creates are legitimate when the constitution has widespread support, effectively protects basic human rights, and generates law according to a procedure that affords all citizens input in determining the common good.[7] In fact, since the list of basic human rights that we discussed in chapter 4 includes a right to participate in the political structure of one's society, this final requirement is technically redundant. The important implication of this account is that when a political structure is legitimate – when basic human rights are protected and there is a mechanism for making collective, explicit, and binding decisions – there is a strong presumption that justice prohibits resisting and interfering with the creation and enforcement of the law. This presumption can be defeated. Sometimes civil disobedience or conscientious refusal may be justified, even when there is a legitimate political structure. However, the clearest cases of justifiable civil disobedience, both historically and theoretically, occur when some basic human right is denied, such as the rule of law or the right to participate in making political decisions (Rawls 1999a: 319–43). To the extent that some basic right is systematically violated, the legitimacy of that regime is undermined, although this may certainly come in degrees.

In general, when a society has a legitimate system of law, it would be unjust to attempt to use force to resist or to change its political structures or laws, even when the laws are substantively unjust. And note that it would be unjust not only for members of that society to resist, but for *anyone* (not only citizens) to attempt to use force to change those political structures. As Waldron observes (with respect to one aspect of a legitimate legal system), "if the criminal justice system of a country is fair, everyone everywhere has a duty not to obstruct it, whether they owe any particular allegiance to that system and live under its laws or not" (Waldron 1993: 10). The kind of toleration that follows, I should stress, concerns the use of force (and threats) and in no way rules out criticism of unjust laws and institutions, whether domestic or foreign. Rawls is explicit on this point:

> Critical objections, based either on political liberalism, or on comprehensive doctrines, both religious and nonreligious, will continue concerning this and all other matters. Raising these objections is the right of liberal peoples and is fully consistent with the liberties and integrity of decent hierarchical societies. (Rawls 1999b: 84)

Rawls objects not to criticism, but to the view that says that injustice can always properly be met with "some form of sanction – political, economic, or even military – depending on the case" (p. 60).[8]

A legitimate political order has mechanisms that allow it to change in response to the will of the people, and therefore people collectively have the capacity to reform their political structures and laws if they so choose. As we have seen, the basic human right to political participation is the right that citizens have to participate in the political decisions that will be imposed coercively in their society.[9] There is, however, no such general right to participate in the decision-making process of other societies, and individuals can properly be excluded from them. This is not to say that foreigners *must* be excluded. We can imagine a legitimate political procedure that allows a formal role for certain neighboring or allied countries or other foreign groups when a proposed law would significantly affect them. But it is not unjust for a constitution to exclude them, and legitimate political processes will typically make this distinction (Kolers 2002).

Consider now the difference between the attitude that it is appropriate for an individual to have toward an injustice in his own society and the attitude that it is appropriate for him to have toward an injustice in another society – assuming that neither injustice violates basic human rights and that both societies have legitimate political institutions. Because his own society has a legitimate political order, he is free to express his opposition to the injustice and also to advocate, through appropriate political mechanisms, that the law be changed so as to address the injustice. There is no guarantee that his objections will prevail, but he is owed a hearing, a good-faith reply, and access to a political mechanism that will result in a change if he successfully makes his case. What he may not do (in general) is attempt to pre-empt the political process through threats or force that go beyond the constitutional law-making procedures. With respect to a corresponding injustice in a foreign society, he is once again prohibited from the use of force or coercion, and he may still criticize the injustice. However, typically there will be no mechanism that grants him access to the political procedures of the foreign country. Despite the fact that the injustices may be analogous, this asymmetry is appropriate. In one case, the individual is a member of the collective body in whose name the injustice is being perpetrated, while in the other case he is not complicit in the injustice.

In our discussion of realism we saw that there is a powerful temptation to follow Hobbes and to draw a close analogy between individuals in a single state and countries in the global order. Yet, there is an important difference that is illuminated by this account of legitimacy. When individuals belong to a legitimate state, although they have a right to participation, they are subject to non-voluntarist coercion by the political institutions of the state. There are limits to this coercion, of course, set in part by basic human rights and the conditions of continued legitimacy of the political structure. Within those limits, however, a state is empowered to enforce the law against an individual, whether or not she has consented to and supports that law. Individuals, in general, can have no veto over the laws of their society (Estlund 2003:

397–9). In the absence of a global state, a just global order has no analogue to that power. As we will see further in chapter 8, within the limits set by basic human rights and the conditions of legitimacy, states are *not* subject to the coercive force of other countries beyond the treaties and declarations to which they consent. Or, more precisely, in a *just* global order, they *wouldn't* be subject to such coercion. They would still, of course, be bound to one another formally through treaties and declarations, and informally through trade and other interactions. But (again, when legitimate political institutions are in place) these can be understood as voluntary in a way that domestic law is not. As long as they remain within the limits set by basic human rights, states are not subject to the coercive force of others, or even of a majority vote of all other states, whereas citizens of a legitimate state are.

As we have seen, justice requires that everyone respect the basic human rights of all people. In that sense, this account is a form of cosmopolitanism. But the possibility of different individuals being members of different legitimate political orders moves us away from the strong cosmopolitanism that we discussed in chapter 3. What is fundamental here is the idea that when a person is subject to the coercive imposition of a legal system, he has a fundamental right to participate through an appropriate mechanism in determining the content of *that* system of law. In chapter 7 we will see another way in which justice distinguishes between foreigners and compatriots who fall under a shared legitimate political order. But now I want to stress that although this account shows how we can move away from strong cosmopolitanism, it does so without slipping into the most common forms of nationalism, also discussed in chapter 3. What is relevant from the point of view of justice is not nationality, ethnicity, culture, or any subjective identification. What matters is the objective fact of citizenship in a legitimate political order. Thus, justice is not tied to any particular conception of the good or comprehensive doctrine; nor does it privilege any particular form of identification over others. We can understand this account of legitimacy as requiring a kind of self-determination among societies that (already) have legitimate political orders. However, it says nothing about which groups are entitled to this self-determination. It does not address how and by whom legitimate political orders should be formed or where state boundaries should be drawn. To that extent it is compatible with the fundamental nationalist claim that state borders should correspond to national boundaries. It is still possible to argue on (quasi-) empirical grounds that a high degree of national identification is desirable or even necessary to achieve a stable and legitimate political order (D. Miller 1995: 93–6).

When we face the question of how state borders should be drawn, it would be utopian in the pejorative sense to consider carving up territories from an imaginary state of nature. That is not a problem we will ever face. Because the current world is already divided into states, the question we must face concerns the possibility of redrawing existing borders. In practice, this typically amounts to answering the question: Does justice allow a determined minority, often a nationalist minority, to break away from an existing state and create a new state of their own? The first step in answering this question is to determine the legitimacy of the political order in the existing state. If it is not legitimate, the case for secession is much stronger. Depending on the severity of violations of human rights in the existing state, there may even be a demand for international military assistance. But support for a secessionist movement also depends on an assessment of the likelihood that the prospective state will be able to establish legitimate political structures that protect basic human rights. One crucial issue concerns the potential treatment of minorities in the new secessionist state. As Ignatieff points out, "Almost all secessionist claims are demands for ethnic majority rule, and, with few exceptions, involve the potential for tyranny over ethnic minorities" (Ignatieff 2003: 309–10; cf. Buchanan 1997: 45; McGarry 1998). Another issue concerns the economic prospects of the remaining state after secession. A secessionist movement that claimed all of the resource-rich territory in an existing state for itself, leaving the remaining state in a condition of poverty, would be unjust. At a minimum, some form of fair compensation, "the international equivalent of alimony and child support" (Walzer 1992: 168), must be negotiated.

Now suppose that the existing state is protecting to a reasonable degree the basic human rights of all of its citizens, and the secessionist minority is not excluded from the political system. Nonetheless, this minority still wants independence.

From the perspective of global justice, assuming that both future states are likely to enjoy legitimacy, there can be no objection to a negotiated and peaceful split. The division of Czechoslovakia into the Czech Republic and Slovakia in 1993 is an important recent illustration of this possibility. Furthermore, it is possible that in some conditions, incorporating a carefully crafted right to secede into a constitution may paradoxically serve to temper factionalism and make actual secession less likely (Weinstock 2001: 194–200).

At the level of theory, the hard case concerns a nationalist minority that wants to secede from a legitimate state, but is unable to secure a negotiated agreement to do so. Here we are asking whether principles of global justice grant a people a non-remedial right to secede. For authors who argue that legitimate political authority can be based only on individual consent, the answer is clearly that there is such a right. On this view, an existing state loses its legitimacy over any individuals who withdraw their consent from it, and these individuals are then free to consent to and create a new state. For consent theorists such as Henry Baron, "secession must be permitted if it is effectively desired by a territorially concentrated group and if it is morally and practically possible" (Baron 1987: 37). In contrast, I have defended an account of legitimacy that does not depend on individual consent. My account is congenial to the "remedial right only" theory of secession defended by Buchanan, according to which "a group has a general right to secede if and only if it has suffered certain injustices, for which secession is the appropriate remedy of last resort" (Buchanan 1997: 34–5; cf. 2004: 353–9, 408–21). The injustices in question must be severe enough to put the legitimacy of the existing state into question, such as serious and persistent violations of basic human rights or a previous unjust annexation of territory (Buchanan 2004: 275–6). Quite simply, the thought is that when a state satisfies the conditions for legitimacy, it may enforce its rule over its territory. Furthermore, a legitimate state generates a duty to assist in upholding its institutions and not to use force in resisting its legitimate rule. But that is exactly what a secessionist movement would be doing. There is, therefore, no general right to secede from a legitimate state. In the absence of special conditions, such as serious injustice that puts its legitimacy into question, a state may properly resist a secessionist movement's use of force. "Where there exist adequate federal guarantees for minority rights in the institutional structure of a country," Ignatieff writes, "there is always a prima facie case to maintain the federation and resist claims to secession" (Ignatieff 2003: 310).

However, there is one complication to which Buchanan is insufficiently attentive. The legitimacy of a state depends on its continued ability to protect basic human rights by, among other things, effectively enforcing the law. Although individual consent is not required for legitimacy, a determined minority may be able to undermine the state's effectiveness (at least in a certain region), and thus put its legitimacy (in that region) in question. At that point the creation of a new state might be the most effective way to establish legitimate rule. Such an account, it will properly be objected, sets up an incentive for secessionists to become radicalized: only by effectively undermining existing legitimate rule does it become morally permissible for them to secede. This is indeed a problem and must be faced. Note, however, that a secessionist movement that undermines the existing legitimate rule of a state by engaging in terrorism or other human rights violations will rarely be in a position credibly to assert that a new state under its leadership would better protect human rights. This leaves one further possibility. If a secessionist movement undermines the effective rule of an existing legitimate state through nonviolent, passive resistance, and it credibly claims that it could form a state that secures human rights for all, then there is a strong case to be made for allowing it to do so.

Three final points are worth making about secession. First, when the rule of law breaks down in so-called failed states, it is a matter of the greatest urgency to establish governments that can impose legitimate rule. This may involve drawing new borders – in effect, creating new states. Doing this appropriately depends on specific knowledge of the prevailing and historical conditions. The focus must be on establishing a political authority that is able to secure basic human rights (Buchanan 2004: 366–9; Ignatieff 2003). Second, those who assert that there is a non-remedial right to secession often put stringent qualifications on the conditions under which such a right may be exercised. In fact, there may be very few actual cases that such a theory would allow secession while a remedial right only theory would not (Philpott 1998: 90). Finally, as Buchanan and others have argued recently, there are often many good reasons for a legitimate state to offer some kind of internal recognition or autonomy to its minority groups that falls short of secession (Buchanan 2004: 402–3).[10]

We must now address what justice requires in the absence of a legitimate political order – when basic human rights are not adequately protected or are systematically violated. As I have argued, there is a general duty to respect and protect basic human rights, and in most cases these rights can be secured only through the creation of legitimate political structures. This means that the core duty of justice is to assist in the creation of legitimate political institutions when they are lacking. Often when legitimate political institutions are lacking, it is because of illegitimate but powerful rulers who, far from protecting human rights, actively violate them. Obviously, in such a case the rulers are far more responsible for the injustice than are those foreigners who stand idly by and allow the abuse to continue. Yet, just as clearly, in some cases assistance from outsiders represents the only hope for the victims. Although a long-term goal must be the creation of a legitimate political structure, often a more immediate objective is to put a stop to the ongoing abuse.

This raises the difficult question of so-called humanitarian intervention, which, as one definition has it, involves "the threat or use of force across state borders by a state (or a group of states) aimed at preventing or ending widespread and grave violations of the fundamental human rights of individuals other than its own citizens, without the permission of the state within whose territory force is applied" (Holzgrefe 2003: 18). It is important to emphasize that not all violations of basic human rights are equally bad. The "soft-authoritarianism" of Singapore must not be confused with the genocidal actions of the Hutus in Rwanda in 1994. Lesser violations require less dramatic responses, ranging from diplomatic protests to suspension of joint military exercises and military sales or trade sanctions and embargoes (although the damage that the latter can inflict should not be underestimated) (Neier 2000; Pierce 1996; Beversluis 1989; Damrosch 1993, 1994; Cortright and Lopez 2002; Martin 1992). To simplify our discussion, however, we will focus on the most extreme response, and ask when humanitarian intervention involving military force is permissible and when, if ever, it is required.

We can take two extreme positions to set the terms of debate. At one extreme, it might be said that a humanitarian intervention is justified when the likely benefits outweigh the likely costs, since when a state violates basic human rights, it loses its legitimacy and forfeits its claim to sovereignty. Jeremy Bentham, for example, held that it would be unjust if "a nation should refuse to render positive services to a foreign nation, when the rendering of them would produce more good to the last-mentioned nation, than would produce evil to itself" (quoted in Holzgrefe 2003: 22; cf. Brandt 1972: 157). If we assume (perhaps contrary to Bentham) that human rights violations have a level of disutility that swamp other considerations, the implication of this view is that humanitarian intervention is justified – indeed, *required* – if it is likely to result in a net decrease in human rights violations. This represents a particularly strong form of cosmopolitanism, since it apparently requires a perfectly impartial concern for all individuals, or more precisely for their utility, regardless of state boundaries. At the opposite extreme are those who argue that virtually no humanitarian intervention is ever justified. Some who make this argument are pacifists, arguing that military force is never justified, whatever the aims or circumstances. More often, however, those who oppose humanitarian intervention make their case in terms of respect for state sovereignty as traditionally understood.

Neither of these extreme positions has a proper regard for basic human rights. Between these extremes there are many more nuanced positions, with many authors attempting to spell out necessary and sufficient conditions for humanitarian interventions to be morally permissible (or required). However, I agree with Tom Farer when he argues: "The perceived legitimacy of future interventions to protect people from state or, for that matter, private terrorists can never be a function of some sort of mechanical compliance with general criteria" (Farer 2003: 79). It is an important point, to which we will return, that any assessment of a particular use of military force will depend heavily on judgments about the specific case. Still, we can identify some general considerations that will always be relevant. The first consideration is the most obvious: since there is an initial presumption against any use of military force, there must be good reason to believe that the proposed intervention will result in more good than harm. Since we must expect virtually every military intervention to result in casualties to innocent civilians, the violations that will be prevented must be very serious and imminent. Thus, as Michael Walzer argues, "Humanitarian interventions are not justified for the sake of democracy or free enterprise or economic justice or voluntary association or any other of the social practices and arrangements that we might hope for or even call for in other people's countries. Their aim is profoundly negative in character: to put a stop to actions that, to use an old-fashioned but accurate phrase, 'shock the conscience' of humankind" (Walzer 2004: 69; cf. Walzer 2000: 107; Coady 2003: 286-7).

Walzer's case is based in part on the argument that "The members of a political community must seek their own freedom, just as the individual must cultivate his own virtue. They cannot be set free, as he cannot be made virtuous, by any external force" (Walzer 2000: 87).[11] Critics who defend more permissive accounts of intervention reply with both empirical and theoretical arguments. On the empirical side, Tesón asserts that "as a matter of history this is simply wrong" (Tesón 1988: 29). There have been many liberation movements that have benefited enormously from outside intervention and likely would have failed without it. Tesón therefore defends a "broad interventionism" that is not limited to cases of "extreme human rights violations, such as genocide, mass murder or enslavement" (pp. 21-2). On the theoretical side, Moellendorf argues: "Suppose that popular struggle is a necessary condition for the maintenance of just institutions after a victorious struggle. It does not follow that victory without any outside assistance is also a necessary condition" (Moellendorf 2002: 114). The critics are right. Sometimes ruthless rulers dominate and abuse their societies to the point that the only possibly effective resistance depends on outside intervention. But there remains a kernel of truth in Walzer's position.

It is important to remember that the ultimate goal is to establish institutional structures that secure basic human rights. The aim must be to "create the state order that is the precondition for any defensible system of human rights and to create the stability that turns bad neighborhoods into good ones" (Ignatieff 2003: 321; cf. Rawls 1999b: 94–101). While foreign intervention may help stop acute humanitarian crises, this longer project requires work (and often assistance) that is not primarily military in nature. Indeed, the long-term project of building institutions that secure basic rights, including most importantly legitimate political structures, may be hindered by the use of outside military force. This is in part because legitimate political institutions need to be seen as legitimate by the people of the society. Citizens must generally believe that the political decisions that are made are, in fact, the collective decisions of their society. It is not impossible that outside military intervention can assist in the creation of such institutions, but more often it may put their legitimacy in doubt. "Colonialism got its bad name," Coady observes, "not merely from the explicitly repressive policies of the colonial powers, grim as they commonly were, but also from the inherent difficulties foreigners face in understanding their subject peoples, in properly comprehending their religious, cultural, and historical circumstances" (Coady 2003: 282). The difficulty of establishing legitimate political structures through outside force can sometimes be mitigated when the use of military force is authorized by what is seen to be a legitimate body (such as the UN Security Council) or a traditional ally, but it is exacerbated when the use of force is from a traditional adversary or when the intentions of the foreign power are questionable.

Unlike Walzer, Darrel Moellendorf (2002) holds that interventions should not be limited to only the most extreme cases. Yet, he wants to resist the purely instrumental attitude that Bentham, for example, defends. Moellendorf holds that in addition to there being a just cause – that is, an injustice "either in the basic structure of the state or in the international effects of its domestic policies" (2002: 118) – three additional criteria must be satisfied in order for humanitarian intervention to be justified. First, "it must be reasonable to believe that the intervention is likely to succeed" (p. 119). Second, the intervention must be a "last resort," pursued only after all other means of addressing the violations have been exhausted. Third, Moellendorf requires "proportionality": "Military interventions ought not to repair an injustice at costs to human well-being even greater than the injustice itself" (p. 120).

These are useful guidelines, but what I want to stress is how far short they fall of anything like a mechanical decision procedure. Each of these criteria, in fact, will depend on controversial judgments in any actual case. For example, as Richard Miller points out, reasonable belief in the likelihood of success is compatible with there also being "a reasonable case for the *non*-likelihood of success" (R. W. Miller 2004b: 474).[12] The "last resort" requirement also is a matter of judgment that will often be controversial. As Moellendorf himself observes: "What counts as a last resort is, however, relative to circumstances. Given an infinite amount of time and no costs associated with delay, no intervention is a last resort. However, there are often significant costs associated with delay, such as lost opportunity or continued perpetration of injustices" (Moellendorf 2002: 119). And finally, when human rights are at stake, there can be no mechanical balancing of proportionality. Moellendorf rightly points out: "Determining whether the evil of an intervention is outweighed by the prospect of remedying an injustice is not a simple matter of measuring evils according to a common standard. . . . The exercise of moral judgment sensitive to the morally salient features of a particular situation is the best that one can expect in these matters" (p. 120).

It is sometimes said that humanitarian intervention must have proper authorization. Although international law may be in a state of flux concerning this matter, authorization generally requires approval by the UN Security Council. This is far from ideal, for many reasons, including the fact that, as Henry Shue points out, the Security Council "is outrageously undemocratic with vetoes in the hands of an odd assortment of five countries, all major powers 50 years ago but similar now mainly in being admitted nuclear powers, including a gargantuan dictatorship with pre-modern delusions about state sovereignty and two faded imperial powers with small populations and insignificant economies" (Shue 1998: 73). There have been numerous proposals for reform or for the creation of some alternative authorizing body, but our issue is with authorization itself, not the specific design of the authorizing body. Moellendorf holds that there are several reasons why obtaining proper authorization is often valuable. However, he holds that they "do not outweigh justice when an otherwise justified intervention fails to receive proper authorization" (Moellendorf 2002: 121). There will always be costs associated with humanitarian intervention, not only financial but also human. Obtaining proper authorization will often help ensure that these costs are fairly dispersed among different countries. In addition, as I argued above, the perceived legitimacy of humanitarian interventions is often crucial for its success. These considerations tell in favor of obtaining proper authorization, but I agree with Moellendorf that they may be outweighed. There is one additional reason for requiring proper authorization, however, and it is a powerful one.

As Richard Miller observes, "For better or worse, militarily powerful governments will be the leading agents in implementing the risky procedure of humanitarian military intervention, the more so the more powerful they are" (R. W. Miller 2003: 227). Even leaving aside cases of deliberate distortion and hypocrisy, we know that the judgment of such governments is likely to be distorted by numerous factors, not least of which is their own self-interest, as well as various other biases and prejudices. The very fact that a country has a powerful military is liable to distort its ability to make clear judgments concerning any set of criteria like the ones Moellendorf presents. This has been demonstrated time and time again, but can be crystallized in the comment that US Secretary of State Madeleine Albright made to Colin Powell, the Chairman of the Joint Chiefs of Staff, during the Bosnian crisis in 1993: "What's the point of having this superb military that you're always talking about if we can't use it?" (Powell with Persico 1996: 561). Countries attempt to rationalize virtually anything in humanitarian terms. As Tom Farer observes:

> Claims to be helping humanity sounded among the hodge-podge of justifications for Europe's nineteenth-century imperial interventions. And whether removing or exterminating Native Americans, acquiring Cuba, suppressing an independence movement in the Philippines, or making Latin America safe for capitalism, the United States has rarely missed an opportunity to invoke humanitarian ends. (Farer 2003: 78)

This raises the importance of distinguishing two questions that might otherwise be thought to have the same answer. On the one hand, we might ask what substantive criteria ought to be satisfied in order for a humanitarian intervention to be morally acceptable in the ideal. Moellendorf's moderate interventionism (perhaps with some modifications) provides a good answer. On the other hand, if we have reason to believe that powerful countries are unreliable in their judgments concerning when these criteria are met, we might also ask what institutional checks and safeguards might mitigate their potentially faulty judgment.

When the input of other countries is required in order to authorize an intervention, it may serve as a check on the biased judgment of countries and their tendency to rationalize their narrow self-interest in humanitarian terms. Walzer expresses doubt that proper authorization can help much in this regard: "States don't lose their particularist character merely by acting together. If governments have mixed motives, so do coalitions of governments" (Walzer 2000: 107). Walzer is right that coalitions of countries, no less than individual countries, always have mixed motives, and that international authorization is no guarantee that a decision will be correct. Nonetheless, international authorization may make a significant difference in separating humanitarian concern from narrow self-interest (Farer 2003: 75–6). It is, therefore, of the utmost practical urgency to develop institutional checks and safeguards that prevent a single country from undertaking military action based on its own judgment of whether the criteria permitting intervention are satisfied. In the end, I am unwilling to say that a country should *never* undertake a unilateral humanitarian intervention. However, this should require essentially incontrovertible proof, presented in public, that there is an "ongoing or imminent genocide, or comparable mass slaughter or loss of life" (Roth 2004: 17).

Finally, we must ask the question whether humanitarian intervention is ever required. The duty of justice, I have stressed, does not only impose a prohibition on the violation of human rights. It also generates positive duties to assist in the creation of new institutions to protect human rights when they do not exist. But this duty has limits, and in general it is unreasonable to insist that individuals who fail to make extreme sacrifices for others are acting unjustly. To be sure, when an individual can rescue another at very little cost to himself, a failure to do so would violate a basic duty toward others. However, when the rescue would be extremely dangerous, refusal to put oneself at great risk (or refusal to put others at great risk) does not involve a violation of justice, even if it would be permissible or admirable to intervene. But the truly difficult questions concern cases in which there is a genuine humanitarian catastrophe that could likely be stopped with a relatively small but not negligible cost in human lives. The problem with holding that intervention is never required is put starkly by Walzer: "Somebody ought to intervene, but no specific state in the society of states is morally bound to do so. And in many of these cases, no one does. . . . The massacres go on, and every country that is able to stop them decides that it has more urgent tasks and conflicting priorities; the likely costs of intervention are too high" (Walzer 2000: p. xiii). Some authors hold that societies will too rarely take up the option to protect the rights of foreigners from the worst kinds of abuses unless there is a duty to intervene. Moellendorf, for example, holds that "there is a prima facie duty to intervene in the affairs of states either with unjust basic structures or whose domestic policies create international injustices" (Moellendorf 2002: 125; cf. Lango 2001).

In contrast, David Luban, who was once a vigorous defender of humanitarian intervention, has recently modified his position, and now argues that although it may sometimes be "shameful" not to engage in humanitarian intervention, there is no obligation to do so: "If there was a genuine obligation to intervene militarily on behalf of the basic rights of foreigners, a people would have no right *not* to go to war when the basic rights of foreigners are imperiled. But a people always has the right not to go to war" (Luban 2002: 94). Since war involves making and/or imposing extreme sacrifices, this seems correct. We must expect that in any humanitarian intervention that relies on military force, some lives will be lost in an effort to protect others. And, as Henry Shue argues, "A requirement that someone sacrifice the enjoyment of his or her own basic rights in order that someone else's basic rights be enjoyed would, obviously, be a degrading inequality" (Shue 1996: 114).

The parties to the 1948 Convention on Genocide committed themselves to preventing the destruction "in whole or in part, [of] a national, ethnical, racial or religious group" (United Nations 1948a). While countries may be within their rights to decline to intervene unilaterally, there is a collective obligation among these countries to do what they can to prevent genocide. One recent grievous failure to fulfill this obligation was the Rwandan genocide of 1994, in which at least 800,000 people were killed out of an original population of around seven and a half million. According to the journalist Philip Gourevitch:

> [T]he UNAMIR [the UN peace-keeping force in Rwanda] commander, Major General Dallaire declared that with just five thousand well-equipped soldiers and a free hand to fight Hutu Power, he could bring the genocide to a rapid halt. No military analyst whom I've heard of has ever questioned his judgment, and a great many have confirmed it. . . . Yet, on the same day, the UN Security Council passed a resolution that slashed the UNAMIR force by ninety percent, ordering the retreat of all but two hundred and seventy troops and leaving them with a mandate that allowed them to do little more than hunker down behind their sandbags and watch. (Gourevitch 1998: 150)

The US played a particularly shameful role behind the scenes in preventing the Security Council from authorizing the necessary peace-keeping force (Gourevitch 1998: 152–4; Power 2002: 329–89). Even if we concede that the US could legitimately have declined to risk the lives of its troops as part of a UN mission, its maneuvering to prevent others from doing so was disgraceful. Unlike the USA, however, other countries, notably Belgium and France, had closer historical ties with Rwanda. Arguably, the legacy of Belgian colonial rule contributed to the ethnic hostility between Hutus and Tutsis. To the extent that this is true, Belgium would seem to have borne a more significant obligation to intervene. As Erin Kelly argues,

> Sometimes clear and direct causal connections can be drawn between the conduct of one state and the human rights situation in another. . . . When the international community reasonably

deems it necessary to intervene across borders in order to halt abuses, those states that have been causally involved with the injustice are obligated to support that effort (with soldiers, supplies and money), when they have the resources to do so. (Kelly 2004: 181)

As a general matter, then, although countries do not have a duty to assist in permissible humanitarian interventions, there may be such a duty if a country has committed itself to provide such assistance or if it bears partial responsibility for the creation of the conditions in which basic rights are violated.

7
Poverty and Development

In chapter 4 I defended an account of basic human rights that included a right to essential resources. As I pointed out in chapter 5, sometimes this right is deliberately violated by rulers who aim to starve or impoverish particular individuals or groups for political reasons. Such policies, if severe enough, may justify external pressure, and in extreme cases potentially humanitarian intervention. But the far more common source of deprivation of this right is simply poverty, which itself has multiple, complicated causes. The focus of this chapter will be primarily not on pressuring regimes to stop depriving people of their rights, but on assisting them in securing them. The duty of justice requires that everyone help to create and to sustain institutions that can protect and provide access to basic human rights, including secure access to essential resources. As I have stressed, the strength of this duty is not the same for everyone. Other things being equal, the duty is stronger among wealthy societies, those that can assist most effectively in the particular case, and those that played a historical role in imposing an unjust social order (for example, through colonialism). Charles Beitz summarizes this approach: "The short of it is that a judgment about who is responsible to act depends on the intersection of considerations of causal responsibility for a deprivation and capacity to intervene effectively" (Beitz 2004: 208).

Unfortunately, it is all too easy to establish that in much of the world the basic human right to essential resources is not secure. Indeed, the extent of deprivation is staggering. In 2001, close to half of the world's population lived on less than $2 per day, calculated on the basis of purchasing power parity (PPP), and over one billion people lived in extreme poverty, defined as less than $1 per day, PPP (Chen and Ravallion 2004: 31, table 4).[1] These thresholds are very low – the $2 per day level is approximately one-tenth of the official poverty level in the USA, for example.[2] Furthermore, according to calculations by Thomas Pogge, "Those below the higher line [$2 per day] fall 43 percent below it on average, and those below the lower line [$1 per day] fall 30 percent below it on average . . . The former are 47 percent of humankind with about one and one quarter percent of global income. The latter are 20 percent of humankind with about one third percent of global income" (Pogge 2004a: 283, n. 21). In effect, this means that about half of the world's population lives on less – often *far* less – than the very poorest citizens of the wealthiest countries.[3] This extreme poverty has predictable results: "Each year, some 18 million [people] die prematurely from poverty-related causes. This is one-third of all human deaths – 50,000 every day, including 34,000 children under age five" (Pogge 2002: 2). Most of these deaths are not due to literal starvation but to increased vulnerability to what would otherwise probably be minor disruptions. Easily treatable diseases become death sentences. For example, according to the World Health Organization, "Approximately 4 billion cases of diarrhea each year cause 2.2 million deaths, mostly among children under the age of five. This is equivalent to one child dying every 15 seconds, or 20 jumbo jets crashing every day" (World Health Organization 2000: box 1.2). Natural disasters such as hurricanes, earthquakes, and droughts inflict their worst damage on those who cling to the edges of life and are unable to cope with even minor changes of fortune. In addition, those suffering from extreme poverty are also the most vulnerable to political oppression and exploitation, as they are unable to fight back against abusive and corrupt rulers. It is hard not to agree with Pogge that "Socioeconomic rights, such as that 'to a standard of living adequate for the health and well-being of oneself and one's family, including food, clothing, housing, and medical care' (*UDHR*, Article 25), are currently, and by far, the most frequently unfulfilled human rights" (Pogge 2002: 91).

Confronted with such appalling numbers, once might reasonably ask whether things are getting better or worse. The answer is mixed, with some areas of great progress but others of significant decline. The UN's *Human Development Report 2003* notes some striking positive achievements: "The past 30 years saw dramatic improvements in the developing world. Life expectancy increased by eight years. Illiteracy was cut nearly in half, to 25%. And in East Asia, the number of people surviving on less that $1 a day was almost halved just in the 1990s" (United Nations Development Programme 2003: 2). These dramatic improvements, especially given the Asian financial crises of 1997–8, are cause for celebration. It is important to remember, of course, that the population of the world continues to increase, so even if the poverty *rate* were held constant, there would be a significant increase in the number of people living in poverty. As David Dollar, an economist at the World Bank, observes:

> Poverty incidence [rate] has been gradually declining throughout modern history, but in general population growth outstripped the decline in incidence so that the total number of poor people was actually rising . . . What is really striking about the past 20 years is that the number of extreme poor declined by 275 million, while at the same time world population rose by 1.6 billion. This decline in the number of poor is unprecedented in human history. (Dollar 2004: 18)

On the other hand, not all trends are positive. Although the number of people living on $1 per day has declined over the last 20 years, the number living on $2 per day or less has actually increased over that time (Chen and Ravallion 2004: 5, 16). Furthermore, most of the global reduction in poverty over the last 20 years has occurred in China, and a large share of that occurred in the early 1980s. Given China's large population, a focus on aggregate levels of poverty on a global scale can hide serious setbacks elsewhere, most dramatically in sub-Saharan Africa where between 1981 and 2001, "The number of poor has almost doubled . . . from 164 million to 316 million living below $1 per day" (Chen and Ravallion 2004:

20). Even the *rate* (and not only the absolute number) of people living in extreme poverty in sub-Saharan Africa has increased over this time, so that by 2001 nearly half of the population lived on less than $1 a day (Chen and Ravallion 2004: table 3). In general, "The number of poor has fallen in Asia [between 1981 and 2001], but risen elsewhere" (Chen and Ravallion 2004: 17; cf. table 3). The *Human Development Report 2003* summarizes its findings this way: "For human development the 1990s were the best of years and the worst of years. Some regions and countries saw unprecedented progress, while others stagnated or reversed" (United Nations Development Programme 2003: 40).

When one is confronted with facts such as these, it is easy to feel overwhelmed by the extent of the problem. It is natural to worry, as the philosopher Richard Rorty puts it, that a significant effort to address global poverty might be so costly that the (formerly) rich might not "still be able to recognize themselves" or "think their lives worth living" (Rorty 1996: 15). This worry fails to recognize that the very large number of poor people is offset by how extremely poor they are. That is, although there are many people suffering from extreme poverty, a relatively small increase in their wealth and income would make an enormous difference to them. To get some sense of the magnitudes involved, consider that according to the *UN Human Development Report 1998*, shifting just 4 percent of the combined wealth of the world's richest 225 people would suffice to "achieve and maintain universal access to basic education for all, basic health care for all, reproductive health care for all women, adequate food for all and safe water and sanitation for all" (United Nations Development Programme 1998: 30, box 1.3). Alternatively, "Shifting merely 1 percent of aggregate global income – $312 billion annually" from the richest countries to the poorest "would eradicate severe poverty worldwide" (Pogge 2002: 2). Now, by itself a large one-time shift in wealth would not solve the persistent problem of poverty. But such numbers do show that the amounts necessary to save millions of people are nowhere near the levels that would endanger the well-being of the wealthiest citizens of the world.

The extreme inequality in global wealth and income in the world today might be thought to be unjust for two very different reasons. First, it might indicate that while there is greater and greater opportunity to fulfill the duty to protect the basic human right to subsistence, it is far from being met. As Pogge observes, "the extent of inequality" may be seen as "a rough measure of the avoidability of poverty and of the opportunity cost to the privileged of its avoidance" (Pogge 2002: 96). A second, distinct conclusion that one might draw is that the inequality is objectionable in itself. That is, it might be thought that it is unjust for some to have significantly more wealth than others, even if everyone had secure access to a threshold level of necessary resources. The human rights approach that I defend accepts the former but not the latter. Global inequality *as such* is not objectionable as long as basic human rights are protected, including secure access to a sufficient supply of basic resources. This position can be seen as an alternative to the position of both the realists, for whom there are no duties of justice owed to foreigners, and also the strong cosmopolitans, who are global egalitarians and hold that principles of domestic justice should apply internationally as well.

Until 1972, few philosophers paid much attention to the moral implications of extreme poverty and inequality, especially across borders. This changed when Peter Singer published an article calling attention to the fact that some nine million refugees fleeing from floods and war in what was then East Pakistan (but was soon to become Bangladesh) were living in horrendous conditions and were in danger of dying "from lack of food, shelter, and medical care" (Singer 1972: 229).[4] From his assumption that "if it is in our power to prevent something bad from happening, without thereby sacrificing anything of comparable moral importance, we ought, morally, to do it" (p. 231), Singer argues:

> it follows that I and everyone else in similar circumstances ought to give as much as possible, that is, at least up to the point at which by giving more one would begin to cause serious suffering for oneself and one's dependents – perhaps even beyond this point to the point of marginal utility, at which by giving more one would cause oneself and one's dependents as much suffering as one would prevent in Bengal. (p. 234)

It is clear from his utilitarianism that Singer does, in fact, favor the stronger conclusion – that we are required to give until we equalize our marginal utility with those who are suffering most in the world (cf. Unger 1996).

I do not believe that Singer's utilitarianism is defensible as a comprehensive moral theory, but it is certainly inadequate as an account of what social justice requires (R. W. Miller 2004a, 2004c).[5] There is no duty of justice to maximize total happiness, nor is there a basic human right to an equal share of resources or of happiness. Moreover, justice does not require that we show perfect impartiality in all aspects of our lives. In many circumstances, it would not be unjust for me to spend my money to improve my daughter's well-being somewhat, even if that money could have made someone else's life much better. There are, however, important limits to the partiality that we are permitted to show to ourselves and particular others. For example, I may not steal from or kill someone else in order to make my daughter's life somewhat better. To do so would be to violate a strong *negative* duty that I have to all people (not to steal from them or to kill them), rather than merely neglecting what is a *positive* duty to help them. In many circumstances, a *positive* duty to help strangers can be overridden by the fact that fulfilling it would be likely to make my (or my daughter's) life worse (even if it is only a little worse), but *negative* duties apply impartially and cannot be overridden as easily.

Recently, some strong cosmopolitans have argued that it is a mistake to view the duty to assist the global poor as merely a positive duty – a matter of charity that can be overridden easily by competing considerations. They argue that the process of globalization, especially the growth of economic trade, has put us into new relationships with people throughout the world, and that these relationships generate stronger duties of justice. There are two questions to consider. First, do these relationships alter the content of the duty of justice? In particular, do they generate egalitarian requirements of distributive justice on a global scale? Second, do these relationships mean that our duties are not merely positive but stronger negative duties? In particular, if we violate them, are we not merely neglecting others but actively harming them?

As we saw in chapter 2, Rawls developed his principles of domestic justice on the assumption that they would be applied to the basic structure of a society. Several authors argue, in effect, that there is now a global basic structure, and if Rawls's egalitarian principles of distributive justice apply domestically, they also should apply globally. Darrel Moellendorf, for example, argues that "Duties of distributive justice . . . arise out of economic association. As capitalism globalizes, it makes more sense to take the primary locus of duties of distributive justice to be the planet rather than the state" (Moellendorf 2002: 72).[6] Since global economic institutions significantly affect everyone's well-being, "duties of justice exist between persons globally and not merely between compatriots" (p. 37). Moellendorf concludes that Rawls's egalitarian principles of fair equality of opportunity and the difference principle ought to be applied globally. He notes that "the present global distribution of resources deviates massively from" the requirements of fair equality of opportunity, and that "Achieving fair equality of opportunity globally would require significant wealth transfers from the wealthiest persons of the developed world to the developing world to support educational, health, food, and security programs" (p. 49). Furthermore, "If fair equality of opportunity alone requires extensive structural changes in the world economy, its conjunction with the difference principles is even more demanding" (p. 81; cf. Caney 2001; Beitz 1999).

There is, however, an important and revealing conceptual difficulty in determining what fair equality of opportunity requires in a global context (Boxill 1987; cf. D. Miller 2004; Caney 2001). To realize fair equality of opportunity, Moellendorf says, a child growing up in rural Mozambique must be just as likely as the child of a senior executive at a Swiss bank "to reach the position of the latter's parent." Taken literally, this would require completely open borders, since there must not be any restrictions on the opportunities of individuals to seek employment anywhere in the world. But Moellendorf does not believe that justice requires open borders (Moellendorf 2002: 66; cf. Carens 1995). What he must have in mind is something closer to this: fair equality of opportunity does not require that a child from Mozambique be as likely as a child of a Swiss banker to reach a senior position in the *Swiss* bank, but rather to be equally likely to reach a *comparable* position in a bank in *Mozambique*. The problem is obvious: what if there is no comparable position in a bank in Mozambique? The difficulty is not simply that the aggregate wealth of the two countries is so different. There can be no moral requirement that the economies of different countries be organized so as to provide precisely parallel employment positions. Moellendorf acknowledges the point, and agrees that the demand for equal opportunity must not require that there be identical positions in each society, but rather positions that have equal shares of financial reward, authority, prestige, security, etc. (Moellendorf 2004: 219). The problem remains, however, because there is no reason to assume that positions in different societies will carry identical or even substantially similar packages of these various goods.

Even if this problem could be overcome by somehow aggregating these various goods into a single measure of "advantage" without relying on any culturally specific interpretation and balance of these goods, it still seems to be too much to demand that the available packages of these goods be equalized across societies. Different societies can evolve in ways that generate positions with different packages of opportunities and goods. Consider two societies with equal aggregate levels of wealth, one of which pursues policies to maintain an egalitarian distribution of wealth while the other allows larger inequalities while guaranteeing all of its citizens a fair opportunity to achieve the higher positions of wealth and providing everyone with an adequate, minimal share. There will not be equal opportunity for the citizens of these two societies, since only those in the inegalitarian society will have the opportunity to achieve the highest positions (while they also face the prospect of falling to a position below those in the egalitarian society). Whether or not we think that the inegalitarian society is inferior from the point of view of domestic principles of justice, surely there is nothing wrong from the point of view of global justice – nothing, that is, that requires the transfer of wealth from one society to the other.

As I indicated, Moellendorf's support for egalitarian principles of global distributive justice follows from his assertion that there is a global economic association of the appropriate kind. Conversely, he holds that in the absence of extensive global economic ties, there would not be global duties of distributive justice (Moellendorf 2002: 36, 37; cf. Pogge 2002: 171). Moellendorf does not indicate how we should measure whether global economic ties are sufficient to generate strong duties of distributive justice; but suppose we look at exports as a percentage of GDP to give us a rough measure of global economic integration. In 1998, exports accounted for 11 percent of the GDP of the United States, 26 percent in the UK, and 11 percent in Japan (World Bank Data Query). How are we to decide whether these levels of integration into the world markets are sufficient to generate a strongly egalitarian duty of justice on a global scale? On the one hand, it seems implausible that there would be a sharp cut-off, say exports of 25 percent of GDP, beyond which such duties are triggered. This would imply that in 1998, the UK, but not the USA or Japan, had a duty of justice to ensure that a global difference principle and fair equality of opportunity were satisfied. An alternative would be to use some kind of graduated scale, reflecting the idea that "The force of responsibility is directly proportional to the degree of association" (Moellendorf 2002: 123). But such an approach has problems, too. For example, between 1996 and 1998, the GDP of South Korea fell by 39 percent, due to the Asian financial crisis. During this same period, its exports as a share of GDP increased from 30 percent to 49 percent. It would be difficult to insist that in these two years, as its economy contracted sharply, South Korea's duty to eliminate global poverty increased by nearly two-thirds.

Furthermore, if trade and foreign investment put wealthy countries under an obligation to relieve the poverty of poorer countries, this would offer a powerful incentive to avoid such interactions, even when they would be useful in reducing poverty. Moellendorf is surely right that the greater economic integration which the world has seen in recent decades calls for new reflection on principles of global justice; but it is not obvious that the proper framework for doing this is simply to assume that the basic structure of society (in Rawls's sense) has been extended beyond state borders. Finally, note that integration into the world economy does not mean that each country interacts with all of the others. It may have extensive trade and investment relations with one (or a few) only. It is unclear why on Moellendorf's view such trade should generate any duty of justice at all toward other countries. It is undeniable that global economic relations often have profound effects on the economies of countries around the world, but this is insufficient to establish that global justice requires the egalitarianism defended by strong cosmopolitans.

In chapter 3, we saw that David Miller holds that basic rights, including a right to a minimal level of resources, are to be protected universally, but that a concern with "material equality" arises only "from membership of various communities and associations, among which the community of citizens in a nation-state is arguably the most important" (D. Miller 1999: 189; cf. 1998a, 2004). The reason why he holds that membership in a nation-state is only "arguably" the most important is because he believes that the egalitarian requirement arises only in communities and associations in which the following is true: "Members must have a shared identity, an awareness that there is something distinctive about them that holds them together in a single unit; there must be common understandings or common purposes that give the community its ethos; and there must be an institutional structure that acts on behalf of the community, in particular overseeing the allocation of resources among the members" (D. Miller 1999: 190). Miller argues that in the contemporary world, it is primarily in nation-states that we find this "shared sense of identity" or "common ethos" (p. 190). For Miller, then, egalitarian distributive requirements exist only among individuals who identify with one another and share a common set of values, since it is only among them that inequality will be experienced as "a failure of recognition and respect." Only within such communities would accepting an inequality "be to declare that those who receive a smaller quota of advantages are not members in full standing but mere adjuncts" (p. 189). Despite the extent of international trade and the existence of international institutions, there is not currently "a world community" that would entitle everyone to equal treatment, because there is not a strong sense of global identity.

As we saw in chapter 3, one of the problems with Miller's account is that it makes the requirements of justice depend on the subjective identification of individuals. The strong cosmopolitans are right that such subjective identification cannot be the grounds on which to distinguish local principles of justice from global principles. Accounts of justice that are dependent on subjective identification are incompatible with the fact that duties of justice are binding "regardless of whether we happen to believe that we are or want to be [bound]" (Moellendorf 2002: 35).[7] That said, we need not agree with the strong cosmopolitans that there is no relevant difference between a domestic basic structure and the global basic structure, or that principles of justice that are appropriate for one must be appropriate for the other. Our discussion of political legitimacy in chapter 6 laid the groundwork for an account that distinguishes the two. Egalitarian principles of distributive justice are grounded not on subjective identification between co-nationals, but on the shared legitimate political structure of fellow citizens.

This approach has been defended recently by Michael Blake, who holds that justice requires a concern with "absolute deprivation abroad and reserve[s] a concern for relative deprivation" among fellow citizens (Blake 2001: 259). Superficially, this may appear similar to Miller's account. But for Blake, the egalitarian demands are due

> not because we care more about our fellow countrymen than we do about outsiders, but because the political and legal institutions we share at the national level create a need for distinct forms of justification. A concern with relative economic shares, I argue, is a plausible interpretation of liberal principles only when those principles are applied to individuals who share liability to the coercive network of state governance. Such a concern is not demanded by liberal principles when individuals do not share such links of citizenship. (p. 258)

As we saw in chapter 2, according to a liberal approach to justice, the coercive imposition of collective decisions must meet a high burden of justification. Specifically, those subject to the coercion must be able reasonably to accept it. Because a political and legal order is imposed coercively on all citizens, it can meet this high burden of justification only when it includes an egalitarian component. Principles of international justice do not have such a high burden to meet, and therefore do not include such an egalitarian distributive requirement.

> In the international arena, by contrast, no institution comparable to the state exists. No matter how substantive the links of trade, diplomacy, or international agreement, the institutions

present at the international level do not engage in the same sort
of coercive practices against individual moral agents. (p. 265)[8]

To make the point more vivid, Blake, like other authors,
including Rawls (1999b: 117), has us imagine two societies
isolated from one another, one relatively wealthy and the
other relatively poor, although "all have enough food to live
a normal and productive life, and no one is in imminent
danger of falling into starvation or objectionable poverty"
(p. 290). When explorers from the poorer society find the
wealthy society, they claim that the inequality is unjust and
that justice requires that some wealth be transferred to them,
arguing that "the fact that we were born on the other side of
the mountain is an accident of fate, and should not be used to
justify the fact of an inequality" (p. 290). Blake claims that the
wealthy society is under no such obligation, and indeed that
even if the societies begin to establish trade relations with one
another, this would not generate egalitarian obligations
between them.

Strong cosmopolitans reject this position, arguing that it is
unfair to hold "Citizens of disadvantaged countries . . . *collectively* . . . accountable for their country's unsound domestic policies, even if they had no part in the making of these
policies" (Tan 2000: 179). But we are assuming that the
society in question has and will retain a legitimate political
structure. Although we cannot expect that every member of
the society will agree with every decision it makes, they are
properly regarded as collective and legitimate decisions of the
society as a whole. Furthermore, there is no reason to believe
that a decision that leads to slower economic advance is necessarily "unsound." There are many perfectly good reasons
why a society might reject policies that aim at maximum
economic growth, ranging from concerns with social disrup-
tion and environmental degradation to "preferring a more
pastoral and leisurely society" (Rawls 1999b: 117). And of
course, societies may freely adopt policies that turn out, in the
judgment of later generations, to have been misguided.
Societies can change their priorities over time, and economic
planning is, after all, far from a perfect science. To deny a
society with a legitimate political structure the ability to make
such decisions for itself, including decisions that others or

even they themselves come to view as mistaken, is simply to deny it and its citizens the ability to self-govern.

In recent years, Thomas Pogge has developed an alternative account of how the global institutional order is coercively imposed on the population of the world without general consent. The existence of such an order is important for Pogge, because he argues as follows: "If the global economic order plays a major role in the persistence of severe poverty worldwide and if our governments, acting in our name, are prominently involving in shaping and upholding this order, then the deprivation of the distant needy may well engage not merely positive duties to assist but also more stringent negative duties not to harm" (Pogge 2004a: 265). Pogge pulls no punches, suggesting that the politicians and diplomats who establish and defend this order are "hunger's willing executioners, committing a rather large-scale crime against humanity in our name" (p. 277). Again, Pogge believes that while we have positive duties to assist those in great need regardless of any causal responsibility for their extreme poverty, we are, in fact, also violating a strong negative duty because we share partial responsibility for causing their poverty (p. 278; cf. 2001: 14).

In order to make his case that the global institutional order is partially responsible for the persistence of extreme poverty, Pogge must overcome the alternative explanatory hypothesis that poverty can be explained *fully* in terms of the domestic features of poor societies. He forthrightly acknowledges that the proximate cause of poverty and underdevelopment in many countries is "a culture of corruption [that] pervades the political system and the economy of many developing countries," which often results in "bad domestic policies and institutions that stifle, or fail to stimulate, national economic growth and engender national economic injustice" (Pogge 2002: 200; cf. 139–40) However, Pogge points out that an explanation that identifies only domestic causes is incomplete, since "it holds fixed, and thereby entirely ignores, the economic and geopolitical context in which the national economies and governments of the poorer countries are placed" (p. 140). In other words, the global factors that Pogge identifies are not independent of the domestic factors; in fact, the former work through the latter. Therefore his analysis does not "lessen the moral responsibility we assign to dictators, warlords, corrupt officials, and cruel employers in the poor countries" (p. 116).

Pogge identifies several ways in which the global order may in some cases facilitate the proximate, local causes of poverty. I will focus on two closely related features that he emphasizes.[9] The first is what he calls the "international resource privilege." Pogge observes that any individual or group that is able to exercise effective coercion over the population in a territory is recognized internationally as entitled to exercise ultimate control over all resources in the territory, regardless of how it came to power or the legitimacy with which it exercises power (Pogge 2002: 140). Among other things, this recognition means that a ruler is entitled to sell "his" property on terms of his choosing. When that happens, "the purchaser acquires not merely possession, but all the rights and liberties of ownership, which are supposed to be – and actually *are* – protected and enforced by all other states' courts and police forces" (p. 113).[10] The second mechanism is analogous. The "international borrowing privilege" allows the *de facto* ruler of a country to "borrow funds in the name of the whole society, thereby imposing internationally valid legal obligations upon the country at large" (Pogge 2002: 114). The fact that anyone who manages to establish control over a country is thereby viewed by the international community as entitled to dispose of his country's resources and to secure loans in the country's name "provides powerful incentives toward coup attempts and civil wars in the resource-rich countries" (p. 113). This is because "Whoever can take power in such a country by whatever means can maintain his rule, even against widespread popular opposition, by buying the arms and soldiers he needs with revenues from the export of natural resources and with funds borrowed against future resource sales" (Pogge 2004a: 270). This allows these illegitimate rulers to focus resources on maintaining their own power, rather than on addressing the pressing needs of their fellow citizens. Furthermore, the country remains responsible for the so-called odious debt that the illegitimate ruler has generated, even after the ruler dies or is deposed (Kremer and Jayachandran 2002). It has been estimated, for example, that "By the time he was overthrown in 1997, [the dictator Mobutu

Sésé Seko] had stolen almost half of the $12bn in aid money that Zaire . . . received from the IMF during his 32-year reign, leaving his country saddled with a crippling debt" (Denny 2004: 12).

Although the debilitating effect of at least some odious debts is undeniable, it is very hard to assess the extent to which the recognition of such regimes contributes to poverty through the mechanisms that Pogge identifies. The argument is supposed to show that recognition of illegitimate regimes contributes to the lack of democracy, and that the lack of democracy, in turn, contributes to the persistence of poverty. While the first link seems intuitively plausible, any assessment of its strength must be highly speculative. There is some evidence that resource-rich countries are statistically less likely to be democratic. An analysis performed by economists Ricky Lam and Leonard Wantchekon found that "a one percentage increase in the size of the natural resources sector [relative to GDP] generates a decrease by half a percentage point in the probability of survival of democratic regimes" (Pogge 2002: 163–4). Pogge's account would provide one possible explanation of this surprising finding, but there are other possibilities. Furthermore, as we discussed in chapter 4, there is little conclusive evidence that democracy contributes significantly to economic development, although since 1960, democratic societies have done at least as well statistically as authoritarian regimes (Halperin et al. 2005).

Even if the mechanisms that Pogge describes are correct, it is not obvious that this establishes that citizens of wealthy countries are violating a negative duty. Because of the institutional dimension, discussed in chapter 4, the case seems to break out of the strict division between negative and positive duties. Furthermore, although the resource and borrowing privileges are imposed on the world, any assessment of the extent to which they are responsible for the persistence of poverty depends on comparing them to an alternative. Such a comparison would not only be speculative, but it is also very difficult to see on what grounds the selection of an appropriate baseline for comparison can be made (Pogge 2002: 136–9, 202–3).

Furthermore, even granting the full strength of Pogge's argument, this is still not enough to establish that the content of the obligation is egalitarian (and Pogge nowhere claims that it does).[11] On Pogge's account, there is a significant difference between how domestic orders contribute to extreme poverty and how the global order contributes. The latter does so through its influence on the former. Domestic institutions contribute to poverty directly through laws and policies that are indifferent to the interests of the majority but that serve the narrow interests of the elite. By contrast, the global order contributes to poverty indirectly, by helping to sustain the illegitimate rule of those who impose these domestic laws and policies. It is reasonable to demand of the global institutions that they help support the creation of legitimate political regimes, or at the very least not help sustain illegitimate rule. By contrast, on the domestic side, where political institutions coercively impose explicit and collective decisions through law, it is appropriate to demand that these institutions satisfy additional egalitarian requirements. So whether or not we agree with Pogge that citizens of wealthy societies contribute significantly to the persistence of global poverty, it remains the case that we can distinguish the content of global principles of justice from the content of the domestic principles. The strength of an obligation must not be confused with its content.

On the institutional approach taken here, the primary duty of justice is to assist in the creation of institutions that protect and secure basic human rights. Although during an acute crisis, there may be an obligation to provide financial or material aid, the long-term aim must be to create self-sustaining institutions. As Rawls observes:

> Well-ordered peoples have a *duty* to assist burdened societies. It does not follow, however, that the only way, or the best way, to carry out this duty of assistance is by following a principle of distributive justice to regulate economic and social inequalities among societies . . . [The] aim is to realize and preserve just (or decent) institutions, and not simply to increase, much less to maximize indefinitely, the average level of wealth, or the wealth of any society or any particular class in society. (Rawls 1999b: 106–7)

Rawls goes on to point out that the "political culture of a burdened society is all-important; and . . . there is no recipe, certainly no easy recipe, for well-ordered peoples to help a burdened society to change its political and social culture"

(p. 108). This seems right: foreign societies have little ability to dictate changes to the political and social culture of a society. On the other hand, as Pogge points out, at least they can stop supporting and sustaining illegitimate regimes through, for example, the resource and borrowing privileges. And to the extent that individuals in wealthy countries have a limited ability to avoid participating in unjust institutional structures, they have a secondary duty to compensate the victims (Pogge 2002: 50).

For the poorest countries, the only way to establish secure access to necessary resources is through economic development and growth. In his Nobel Lecture, Simon Kuznets defines economic growth as "a long-term rise in capacity to supply increasingly diverse economic goods to its population, this growing capacity based on advancing technology and the institutional and ideological adjustments that it demands" (Kuznets 1973: 165). As this definition implies, economic development cannot be captured by focusing on a narrow measure such as per capita income. A society's ability to provide for its population is dependent on institutional and ideological conditions that reach far beyond any simple macro-economic policy. On the other hand, economic development should not be conflated with the requirements of justice itself or the ideal of a good society. Indeed, it should not be assumed that an increase in economic development necessarily contributes to an increase in justice. It would be a mistake to suppress this empirical issue by adopting an over-inclusive definition of economic development (Bardhan 1993: 47).

Economic development is typically measured in the aggregate, but an overall increase in the wealth and productive capacity of a society need not work to everyone's advantage. In fact, Kuznets hypothesized that at low levels of economic development, growth would initially lead to greater inequality, as the relatively well-off are able to take advantage of new opportunities and the relatively poor are left behind (Kuznets 1955). The empirical evidence has not confirmed this as a general pattern, but the issue remains controversial. One recent study of a large sample of 92 countries over four decades finds that the "Average incomes of the poorest fifth of a country on average rise or fall at the same rate as average incomes" (Dollar and Kraay 2002: 218). In other words, as a country experiences economic development and average incomes rise, the income of the poorest fifth rises at the same rate as the average income in the country – income inequality does not tend to increase.[12] This is not to say that income distributions are unchangeable or that efforts to reduce inequality might not help the poor. In their conclusion, the authors emphasize:

> Our findings do not imply that growth is all that is needed to improve the lives of the poor. Rather, we simply emphasize that growth on average does benefit the poor as much as anyone else in society, and so standard growth-enhancing policies should be at the center of any effective poverty reduction strategy. (p. 219)

Economic development need not increase inequality, and indeed it is possible for it to work to everyone's advantage.

The most effective strategies to promote economic development are controversial and uncertain. Furthermore, poor countries often find themselves forced to make a choice between the urgent demands of short-term relief and long-term development (Kitching 2001: 144). In some cases, outside assistance can help a country break out of this conflict, and this can be done without excessive sacrifices on the part of the wealthy. In other cases, unfortunately, the existing government is corrupt or uninterested in addressing poverty in a serious way. In such cases, the primary problem concerns political legitimacy and not only development.[13] In more favorable circumstances, however, when legitimate political structures are in place, there are many possible mechanisms for raising these resources and for distributing them to the people in greatest need.

It is important that efforts aimed at immediate relief – both the raising of funds and their distribution – be designed in such a way that they do not interfere with and, if possible, assist in achieving long-term goals, including development. Not long ago, one issue would have dominated a discussion of the unintended side-effects of relief: the effects on population. In the late 1960s and 1970s, neo-Malthusian arguments were very common. One of the most famous proponents of this position, Garrett Hardin, argued that in the long run, providing food assistance to poor countries would be counter-productive, since aid would decrease mortality rates and thus increase the population, creating even more people in extreme poverty. Without the harsh medicine of starvation, "poor countries will not learn to mend their ways, and will suffer progressively greater emergencies as their populations grow" (Hardin 1996: 10; cf. Ehrlich 1968). Better to let some die now, he argued, rather than to help them survive and create even greater crises in the future.

This argument is not made as frequently today. Only a hideous morality would say that one should not save a life now because doing so might result in other deaths in future generations. Fortunately, the evidence suggests strongly that this is unlikely to be the result. On the narrow issue of food, technological innovations have led to increases in food production that easily outstrip population increases: "Not only is there no real decline in world food production per head (quite the contrary), but also the largest per capita increases have come in the more densely populated areas of the third world (in particular, China, India and the rest of Asia)" (Sen 1999: 205). More generally, the relationship between economic development and population is quite complex. When the so-called Mortality Revolution began in northwestern Europe in the late nineteenth century, average life expectancy at birth was around 35 years. In less than a century, it had doubled to 70 years. This dramatic change was brought about primarily by lowering the very high rates of infant mortality (Easterlin 1996: 7–8). But with the decrease in infant morality, there has also been a significant decrease in fertility rates. As the economist and demographer Richard Easterlin notes:

> The historical experience of the developed countries . . . raises doubts about the concerns of population explosionists [those who predict a population explosion]. In country after country in which mortality fell, fertility followed, a pattern characterized by demographers as the "demographic transition." Sometimes there is an interval when fertility rises because of improvements in fecundity due to better health or reduced breast-feeding. But, in time, in *all* countries experiencing the Mortality Revolution, there was a fertility revolution too. (p. 10)

In short, there is no reason to accept the view that providing assistance to those in great need will result in a population explosion and greater humanitarian crises in the future. As Sen notes, "There can be little doubt that economic and social development, in general, has been associated with major reductions in birth rates and the emergence of smaller families as the norm" (Sen 1994: 64). The most effective (not only morally appealing) strategy in controlling population growth and in reducing future starvation is to spur economic development and to empower women through economic opportunity, education, and birth control.

Far more serious than concerns about population growth is the likely effect of economic development on the environment, including production of greenhouse gases that affect global warming (Gardiner 2004). We cannot discuss these matters in any detail, but it is important to note that as countries develop economically, they become more efficient in their energy consumption. Despite this increased efficiency, however, consumption of energy increases even more rapidly, and thus economically developed countries produce vastly greater amounts of greenhouse gases per capita than do poor countries (Marland and Boden 1996; Singer 2002: ch. 2). To counter this, one of the strategies that Pogge introduces to raise money for the global poor would have environmentally beneficial side-effects. There are many possible variations on Pogge's idea of a "Global Resource Dividend" (GRD), but the basic idea is that each country would continue to have the authority to decide whether and how the raw materials available in its territory would be extracted and used. However, if resources were consumed or sold, the country would have to pay a small percentage, for example 1 percent of its value to a fund to relieve severe poverty globally (Pogge 1998; 2002: ch. 8; J. Mandle 2000a). Modeled on the idea of preferred stock, this would reflect the collective ownership stake of the global population in the world's natural resources. "Under my proposal, the Saudis, for example, would continue fully to control their crude oil reserves. They would not be required to pump oil or to allow others to do so. But if they did choose to do so, they would be required to pay a linear dividend on any crude oil extracted, whether for their own use or for sale abroad" (Pogge 1998: 511). Pogge proposes the GRD primarily as a source of revenue to help the desperately poor. Such a proposal would, of course, raise prices on raw materials as the countries that extract natural resources would no doubt pass on a considerable part of their cost to consumers. Pogge estimates that a $2 per barrel GRD on crude oil extraction alone (approximately 4.75 cents per gallon) would generate approximately $50 billion annually (Pogge 1998: 512). Such a policy would not only benefit the poor, but would also contribute to environmental conservation by creating a greater incentive to conserve and to substitute more renewable and less polluting alternative sources of energy.

I have argued that the human right to subsistence generates both negative and positive duties, as well as institutionally mediated duties that share some features with both negative and positive duties. But I have rejected the claim that this right generates any egalitarian duties of global distributive justice. It is only a shared political structure that raises duties of justice beyond a concern with basic human rights. In the absence of a global state or equivalent political structure, one has fulfilled one's obligations to foreigners when one has assisted in securing their access to basic rights, including subsistence resources. Other moral obligations may exist, of course, but these are not generated by basic human rights and are not obligations of global justice. A final point to emphasize is this: there is considerable common ground available to liberal nationalists, strong cosmopolitans, and the more moderate cosmopolitanism I have defended here.

A UN conference in March 2002 in Monterrey, Mexico, was only the latest time that the countries of world reaffirmed the goal of having wealthy countries provide 0.7 percent of their GNP in foreign direct assistance (United Nations Development Programme 2003: 145).[14] Such levels are not unprecedented. Between 1948 and 1951, the USA, through the Marshall Plan, provided $13 billion to assist in the reconstruction of Europe. At the time, this amounted to approximately 1.52 percent of GDP – more than twice the 0.7 percent level.[15] In recent years, however, only Norway, Denmark, the Netherlands, Luxembourg, and Sweden have allocated Official Development Assistance at a level of 0.7 percent or higher of GDP (Organization for Economic Cooperation and Development 2004). The aggregate levels of assistance are far below this level, and they have declined from 0.33 percent in 1990 to 0.25 percent in 2003 (United Nations Development Programme 2003: 146; Organization for Economic Cooperation and Development 2004). Although providing the largest amount in absolute terms among members of the OECD, the USA gives the smallest amount as a percentage of its GDP – 0.14 percent in 2003 (Organization for Economic Cooperation and Development 2004). Furthermore, a large share of this money is allocated on the basis of strategic political considerations, rather than judgments concerning where it would most usefully meet basic needs (Alesina and Dollar 2000: 33). For example, approximately one-third of US foreign direct assistance goes to only two countries: Israel and Egypt (p. 55). There is room to debate whether and how strategic considerations should influence the allocation of resources, but such funding should not be confused with development assistance aimed at the relief of extreme poverty. Pogge calculates that "All high-income countries together . . . spend about $4.65 billion annually on meeting basic needs abroad – 0.02 percent of their combined GNPs, about $5.15 annually from each citizen of the developed world" (Pogge 2002: 207). Furthermore, "If the other affluent countries spent as much on ODA [Official Development Assistance] as [the five that met the 0.7 percent level] and focused their ODA on poverty eradication (notably including basic health care and education), then severe poverty worldwide could be essentially eliminated by 2015, if not before" (Pogge 2004b: 388).

There is little doubt that wealthier countries could do far more to relieve extreme poverty with at most only minor effects on their ways of life. In fact, the economic development of poor countries can work to the benefit of wealthy countries – economic development is not a zero-sum game. Therefore, there is a sense in which detailed debates about the precise shape of the requirements of justice may seem merely academic, since on any plausible account justice requires that we provide more than our current levels. It is only a failure of political will, based perhaps on a failure of moral imagination – a refusal to look carefully at the effects of our actions and inaction – that prevents us from doing so. This failure of political will may become more and more dangerous, not only for poor countries but for wealthier ones as well. As Pogge observes:

> The times when we could afford to ignore what goes on in the developing countries are over for good. Their economic growth will have a great impact on our environment and their military and technological gains are accompanied by serious dangers, among which those associated with nuclear, biological, and chemical weapons and technologies are only the most obvious. (Pogge 2002: 212)

It may be naive to believe that poverty itself causes terrorism, but it would be equally shortsighted to assume that the indifference of the wealthier countries to the plight of the global poor does not contribute to growing resentment and anger.

8
Globalization

From the point of view of global justice, the process of globalization presents both a challenge and an opportunity. In this final chapter, we will examine some aspects of this process and consider a model of just globalization. Although many theorists characterize the last few decades as an era of globalization, it is often unclear what exactly this is supposed to mean. The process of globalization has many different aspects, but it is helpful to begin by focusing on its economic dimension. The economist Jagdish Bhagwati defines economic globalization as "integration of national economies into the international economy through trade, direct foreign investment (by corporations and multinationals), short-term capital flows, international flows of workers and humanity generally, and flows of technology" (Bhagwati 2004: 3). Perhaps surprisingly, when we look at several of these dimensions of economic integration, such as international trade, foreign direct investment, and labor migration, it turns out that current levels of integration are not so different from the period before World War I. In fact, by some economic measures, the current international economy is *less* integrated than it was a century ago (Kitching 2001: 18; Weiss 1998: 171; Baker et al. 1998: 5; Quiggin 2001: 57). The second half of the twentieth century saw increases in trade, foreign direct investment, and migration, but these increases only returned us to approximately the levels that existed before the turn toward economic isolationism in the first half of the century (especially during the World Wars and the Depression).

These numbers, however, do not adequately capture several important differences between the current globalization and the integration that existed a century ago in the pre-World War I era. Technological developments in several different areas have been important, but the most fundamental difference is due to what has been called the "information revolution." Computer technology, in particular, has led to dramatic changes in how information is processed, managed, and transmitted. Gavin Kitching properly points out that global economic integration will always face limits, since there will always be costs associated with "moving heavy physical things (including people)" (Kitching 2001: 110). By the same token, however, it has now become possible to move immense amounts of *information* virtually anywhere in the world instantaneously and at a very low cost. Not only can people acquire the knowledge necessary for modern economic production, but, more generally, they can find out about profoundly different ways of life. This new information may lead them to reflect on their own ways of life and consider possible changes to their beliefs and aspirations as well as to their social, political, and economic relations with others.

In addition to the information revolution, there are important institutional differences between the current global economic order and the one that prevailed a century or even half a century ago. The post-war global economic order designed at a conference held in Bretton Woods, New Hampshire, in 1944, included the International Monetary Fund (IMF) and the International Bank for Reconstruction and Development (later, the World Bank). The IMF was designed to assist countries by providing short-term loans when they had difficulty meeting their balance of payment obligations due to an economic downturn. The International Bank for Reconstruction and Development was designed primarily to provide long-term loans to assist in the rebuilding of Europe after the devastation of war, but it was largely eclipsed in this role by the USA through the Marshall Plan.[1] Having established the IMF and International Bank for Reconstruction and Development, agreement was reached in 1948 to establish an International Trade Association. However, the US Senate rejected the agreement, and the association never came into existence. Instead, a series of eight rounds of trade negotiations occurred between 1947 and 1994, under the umbrella of the General Agreement on Tariffs and Trade (GATT). A crucial element of this global economic system was "the creation of a system of fixed exchange rates among the major currencies of the world, maintained in place by the power of the postwar U.S. dollar, and by fairly strict capital and exchange controls maintained by all the other major economies of the world, except the United States" (Kitching 2001: 52–3).

The Bretton Woods system was remarkably successful through the 1950s and 1960s. During this "long boom, not only did output and income grow more rapidly on a world scale than ever before, but the real incomes and standards of living of a minority of people on this planet (basically the populations of North America, Western Europe, and Japan) rose more rapidly and more consistently than at any other period in human history" (Kitching 2001: 24). In 1971, the USA abandoned the commitment to convert the dollar to gold at a fixed rate. Although there was some effort to keep exchange rates fixed, that ultimately proved untenable. The floating of currencies meant that new markets were created in currencies themselves, as speculators and businesses hedging against fluctuations were able to bet on future changes in exchange rates. A detailed exploration of the development of global financial markets would take us far beyond the scope of this work. (A useful overview is found in chapters 5 and 6 of Kitching 2001.) However, notice that financial transactions obviously do not require the movement of heavy objects, and that today they can be conducted instantaneously from anywhere in the world. Not surprisingly, international financial markets grew very rapidly in the 1980s and 1990s.

During the post-war period, agreements negotiated under the auspices of the GATT lowered tariffs and quotas that had made trade more expensive. The eight rounds of multilateral negotiations under the GATT succeeded in reducing average industrial tariffs among its members from 40 percent to 3 percent (K. Jones 2004: 4). Furthermore, between the completion of the first round of negotiations in 1948 and the completion of the final round in 1994, the number of member countries expanded from 23 to 128 (K. Jones 2004: 79, table 4.1). There were, however, structural limitations inherent in the GATT.

> The GATT did not establish truly free trade. Signatories to the GATT were not compelled to reduce their tariffs to zero. Instead, in the GATT process, nations were called upon to negotiate mutual tariff reductions with their chief trading partners. Once these downward adjustments had been made, the terms of the GATT agreement stipulated that participating countries extend those same – reduced – tariffs to all other participants. This was described as the extension of most favored nation privileges. (J. R. Mandle 2003: 12)

The final round of GATT negotiations in 1994 ended this *ad hoc* approach by creating the World Trade Organization (WTO) as a successor organization.

The WTO is essentially a forum for multilateral trade negotiations, where all the parties negotiate terms of trade under a single set of rules applicable to all members. The WTO also includes a Dispute Settlement Body (DSB) to resolve trade conflicts among members. "Previously, under the GATT, when a dispute settlement panel sent its recommendations to the GATT council for approval, the proposed settlement had to be unanimously accepted to become binding. This unanimity rule all but stripped the GATT of enforcement power. The nation against which the panel ruled was able to exercise a veto over a proposed settlement" (J. R. Mandle 2003: 32). The WTO includes no such veto provision. On the other hand, it is important not to over-estimate the enforcement power of the WTO. If it finds a country to be in violation of its agreement, the *most* the WTO can do is to authorize the aggrieved country to impose compensatory measures in the form of its own tariffs equal to the damage that it found. Beyond such authorization, the WTO has no power to enforce its rulings. In practice, the actual imposition of such compensatory tariffs is rare. The threat of sanctions is usually sufficient to get countries to enter into negotiations to resolve a dispute.

All of these features – the information revolution, global financial markets, and the WTO – sharply distinguish the current wave of globalization from the situation a century ago. Furthermore, international trade in goods, facilitated by the GATT and WTO and by reductions in transportation costs, has a different character than it did in the past. In addition to trade in finished commodities, there is much greater interdependency in the production process itself. Production is much more dispersed than it has ever been. Multinational corporations are surely the most visible symbols of globalization, but the interdependence at issue does not depend exclusively on them. Even if there were no multinational corporations, producers would still contract out parts of the production process to other companies in other parts of the world. This is done, obviously, because different elements of production are less expensive when carried out in different locations. The scale of this dispersion of production represents a significant increase in global economic integration.

The vast majority of economists believe that the expansion of markets in goods and services is a good thing, at least in general and in the aggregate. To understand why, consider one of the reasons for relying on markets in the first place. Today, virtually all theorists believe that market-based economies are far more efficient than bureaucratically planned economies. Even a self-described "radical egalitarian" defender of democratic socialism like Kai Nielsen holds that "To maximally achieve the meeting of people's needs, we need a market economy" (Nielsen 2003: 49). He continues that at least "many smaller-scale industries" must "operate within market parameters and thus within the discipline of the market. If they operate inefficiently they can and should be allowed to go under" (p. 61). It is the discipline of the market and the credible threat of going out of business if one cannot compete that leads to greater efficiency in the production and distribution of goods and services. In general, a market's growth leads to greater competition, which results in lower prices and the spurring of innovations that increase productivity. The overall result is an increase in real aggregate wealth. An increase in aggregate wealth, however, does not imply that every individual gains. In a system where one firm succeeds and another is allowed to go under, there will inevitably be inequalities. To be sure, these inequalities can and should be mitigated through social welfare programs, but they cannot be eliminated altogether without undermining the efficiency gains that markets generate.

An appreciation of the fact that markets can be important tools for increasing real wealth does not imply that one must be a "market fundamentalist" and adopt a *laissez-faire* approach in which market outcomes are taken as untouchable. After all, justice rarely requires the maximization of aggregate wealth and sometimes is incompatible with it. Other important goals may require embedding market relations within broader non-market political and social institutions. For example, the inequalities that markets generate may be limited in the name of egalitarian considerations, even if this means some sacrifice in overall wealth maximization. In addition, economists recognize many forms of market failure, including "externalities" in which markets under- or over-supply some commodity relative to the socially optimal level, and the formation of monopolies. Furthermore, in order for markets to be beneficial, there are numerous essential background conditions that must be satisfied. As Pogge observes,

> Even truly free markets would probably not bring rapid economic growth to areas where basic infrastructure is lacking and where the physical and mental development of prospective employees has been irreparably impaired through disease, malnutrition, and illiteracy. In such areas a special effort, not purely market driven, is needed to jump-start development. It is only after people there have access to adequate food and shelter, vaccines, safe water, basic sanitation, basic health services, and primary education that these poorest areas will attract significant private investment, which may then be sufficient to sustain and continue the advance on its own. This is not an argument against globalization. But it does show that the developed states must remove their protectionist barriers and make a considerable non-market-driven effort to get the poorest quartile to the point where they, too, can benefit from globalization. (Pogge 2001: 13)

For these and other reasons, carefully designed institutions and social policies are necessary in order to ensure that markets function in ways that work to everyone's advantage. Market fundamentalists dogmatically dismiss such concerns.

Some critics of globalization argue, in effect, that the process of expanding international markets should be reversed. The authors of *Alternatives to Economic Globalization*, for example, argue that "It is necessary to create new rules and structures that consciously favor the local" (International Forum on Globalization 2002: 60). Specifically, "Whenever economic production, labor, and markets can be local, they should be, and rules should help achieve that. International, regional, and sub-regional trade will continue to exist, of course, but it should serve as a final resort, not as the purpose of the system" (p. 107). Presumably, this would require rules and structures that favor local goods even when they are more expensive and would allow imports only "as a final resort," presumably when the goods *cannot* be produced locally at all. They neglect to mention, however, that any society pursuing such a policy will have to endure a tremendous reduction in real wealth. As Kitching points out,

> In the short to medium term then, a breakdown of this glob-alized production structure would have catastrophic implica-tions for the real standard of living of hundreds of millions of ordinary consumers around the world. They would, overnight, lose access to goods (and actually quite a few services) they now take for granted as part of their normal standard of living. Of course, given time it might be possible, by processes of invention and investment, to substitute locally produced prod-ucts for these globalized products. But even if that happened, it could only happen through a large rise in the price of these locally produced substitutes. (Kitching 2001: 30)

Rich societies may be able to afford the luxury of a dramatic reduction in their real standard of living if they choose to favor the local, but this would be devastating for poor soci-eties. Fortunately, there is little evidence for the claim that "a return to the local is inevitable" (International Forum on Globalization 2002: 107).

Instead of blithely advocating policies that will result in sig-nificant reductions in already low standards of living, what is necessary is to develop policies that will allow all people to take advantage of the wealth-creating power of markets. As a 2002 report from Oxfam points out:

> History makes a mockery of the claim that trade cannot work for the poor. . . . If developing countries increase their share of world exports by just five percent, this would generate $350 bn – seven times as much as they receive in aid. The $70 bn that Africa would generate through a one percent increase in its

share of world exports is approximately five times the amount provided to the region through aid and debt relief. . . . [A] one per cent increase in world-export share for each developing region could reduce world poverty by 12 per cent. The decline would be greatest in sub-Saharan Africa and South Asia, the two regions with the highest concentrations of poverty. (Oxfam 2002b: 8–9)

Far from turning one's back on the wealth-creating potential of global markets, anyone truly concerned about the fate of the world's poor must find some way to make them work for the poor. One can advocate reforms or alternatives to current policies and institutions without rejecting globalization or the expansion of markets as such.

In fact, in some cases it is clear that the expansion of competitive markets has not gone far enough to assist the global poor. Consider, for example, the "protectionist barriers" imposed by developed states that Pogge mentions in the quote above. As he writes elsewhere, "My complaint against the WTO regime is not that it opens markets too much, but that it opens *our* markets *too little* and thereby gains for us the benefits of free trade while withholding them from the global poor" (Pogge 2002: 19). This contention is supported by numerous analyses. Consider Oxfam's summary of its 2002 report, entitled *Rigged Rules and Double Standards*: "When developing countries export to rich-country markets, they face tariff barriers that are four times higher than those encountered by rich countries. Those barriers cost them $100bn a year – twice as much as they receive in aid" (Oxfam 2002b: 5).

Even more significant than these tariffs is the fact that farmers in the USA and the EU are able to sell their products below their production cost since they benefit from large agricultural subsidies. This practice, called "dumping," makes it far more difficult for farmers from poor countries to compete, since, lacking their own subsidies, they cannot lower prices below cost. In fact, the magnitude of the EU and US subsidies and their effects on poor countries are startling. "Total OECD agricultural subsidisation exceeds the total income of the 1.2 billion people living below the [$1 per day] poverty line" (Oxfam 2002b: 113). These subsidies also dwarf the foreign direct assistance that OECD countries provide – in 2001, $311 billion compared to $52 billion (United Nations Development Programme 2003: 156). In the USA alone, the 2002 Farm Bill allocated up to $190 billion over 10 years, an increase of 75 percent over previous levels (Mittal 2002). At the end of 2004, *The New York Times* reported that "despite the fact that farm income has doubled in two years, federal subsidies have also gone up nearly 40 percent over the same period – projected at $15.7 billion this year, and $130 billion over the last nine years" (Egan 2004).[2] Overall, industrialized countries provide their domestic farmers more than $1 bn a day, allowing EU and US farmers to export "at prices more than one-third lower than the costs of production" (Oxfam 2002b: 11).

The results of these subsidies are often catastrophic for poor countries, even if they are entirely predictable. According to the World Bank, "OECD tariffs and subsidies cause annual losses in welfare of almost $20 billion in developing countries, equivalent to almost 40 percent of aid in 1998" (World Bank 2001: 11). To choose just a single example, according to Joseph Stiglitz, "subsidies to 25,000 American cotton farmers exceed the value of what they produce and so depresses cotton prices that it is estimated that the millions of cotton farmers in Africa alone lose more than $350 million each year. For several of Africa's poorest countries, losses from this one crop exceed America's foreign aid budget for each of these countries" (Stiglitz 2003: 253–4). To repeat, the criticism here is not that the expansion of markets has harmed the poor. Rather, it is that the current globalization regime has not opened markets in those areas where poor countries could profitably compete (especially in labor-intensive areas such as agriculture and textiles), while at the same time it has forced poor countries to open markets in areas where wealthy countries have an advantage (such as in capital and financial markets). To understand how this has occurred, we must return briefly to the structure of the institutions that manage globalization.

Countries become members of the WTO because they believe that doing so is more economically advantageous than not being a member. Member countries can withdraw from the WTO for any reason with only six months notification

(K. Jones 2004: 85). Currently, membership stands at 148 countries. The WTO aims to reach agreements by consensus, and although it is technically possible to implement an agreement by majority vote, this has never been done. Officially, member states have equal voting power, but, as Kent Jones observes, "in reality, most significant negotiating activities take place behind the scenes, and larger, usually richer countries broker deals on the most important issues" (p. 26). Jones, who is a defender of the WTO, points out that there is an even greater imbalance in dispute settlement proceedings, since poor countries often lack the experts and technical skills to make strong cases (p. 88). In fact, according to one study, "Among developing countries in the WTO, 70 percent have missions that are in some way handicapped by underfunding" (p. 164). Given this imbalance, it is not surprising that negotiations on tariff reductions have concentrated on those areas that would be most beneficial to wealthy countries. Important negotiations aimed at reducing agricultural and textile subsidies in wealthy countries occurred during the ministerial meetings held in Cancún, Mexico, during September 2003. However, it became clear that wealthy countries were only willing to agree to lower their subsidies if poorer countries lowered or eliminated restrictions on foreign investment. In the end, a coalition of developing countries – the G-22, which included China, India, and Brazil – were unwilling to give up their ability to control capital investments in their countries, and the talks collapsed without an agreement.

It is crucial to recognize the difference between the liberalization of trade (the lowering of tariffs, quotas, and subsidies) and financial liberalization. Although there is widespread consensus among economists in support of trade liberalization, there is no analogous consensus about whether liberalization of investment and of financial transactions are comparably beneficial. In fact, as Jagdish Bhagwati, one of the leading defenders of free trade, complains, "the ideas and the ideology of free trade and its benefits . . . have, in effect, been hijacked by the proponents of capital mobility" (Bhagwati 1998: 11). Some defenders of financial liberalization argue that expanding financial markets will result in more capital flowing to underdeveloped countries and therefore more rapid development. But the empirical evidence does not support such predictions – financial liberalization has not, in fact, resulted in capital flows from rich to poor countries. On the contrary, "The U.S.'s rate of capital inflow is now the largest of any country, anytime, anywhere," approximately one-third of which, some $90 billion, "can be attributed to inflows from the developing world" (DeLong 2004: 4). In addition, liberalized financial markets have a strong tendency to exacerbate financial crises.[3] This was most clear in the 1997–8 Asian financial crises. Joseph Stiglitz writes that "capital account liberalization was *the single most important factor leading to the crisis*" (Stiglitz 2003: 99).

While GATT negotiations produced an agreement on Trade-Related Investment Measures (TRIMs) in 1994, during the 1980s and 1990s it was the IMF and the World Bank that were instrumental in opening financial markets. Since they do not operate on the basis of equal voting rights, the policies of the IMF and the World Bank are largely dictated by wealthy countries, which are able to impose conditions that developing countries must meet in order to qualify for assistance. Often these conditions reflect a free-market fundamentalism. No one denies that the "structural adjustment programs" that the IMF and World Bank insisted on in the 1980s and 1990s often led to a short-term worsening of conditions, but defenders argue that this was necessary in order to achieve long-term growth. In fact, there is precious little evidence to suggest that following these policies helped long-term growth. On the contrary, in many cases, countries that resisted IMF conditions did better than those that accepted them. "Today," Stiglitz writes, "even the IMF agrees that it has pushed [liberalization] too far – that liberalizing capital and financial markets contributed to the global financial crises of the 1990s and can wreak havoc on a small emerging country" (Stiglitz 2003: 59). "It is no accident," he continues, "that the two largest developing countries spared the ravages of global economic crisis – India and China – both had capital controls" (Stiglitz 2003: 125).

There is no consensus concerning which, if any, forms of capital controls are beneficial, and we cannot here consider their advantages and disadvantages. But one specific proposal merits special attention: first, because it requires international implementation, and second because (like Pogge's GRD) it illustrates how side-effects can be harnessed for beneficial purposes. After the collapse of Bretton Woods, foreign exchange markets, in which currency is bought and sold, grew dramatically. In 1973, market turnover was approximately $15 billion per day. By 2001, it was approximately $1,200 billion per day, or an annual total of approximately $300,000 billion, equivalent to approximately ten times the entire world's output in goods and services that year (Kapoor 2004: 13). One analysis found that "40% of all [such currency] transactions involve round trips of fewer than three days," and there is evidence that "80% of foreign exchange transactions involve round trips of seven days or less" (Kasa 1999; Tobin 1996: p. xii; Kapoor 2004: 14). Such short-term, speculative investments are sometimes referred to as "hot money." Although few economists think that by itself such speculation causes economic downturns, there is widespread agreement that it can exaggerate the severity of boom and bust cycles (Stiglitz 2003: 17).

In a 1972 lecture, the Nobel laureate economist James Tobin called for a small tax on international currency transactions in order to throw "sand in the wheels" of speculative investments.[4] Because it would be small, less than 0.1 percent on most proposals, it would be felt most by short-term speculators and would do little to impede long-term capital investors. As Tobin writes, "the essential property of the transactions tax – the beauty part – [is] that this simple, one-parameter tax would automatically penalize short-horizon round trips, while negligibly affecting the incentives for commodity trade and long-term capital investments" (Tobin 1996: p. xi). Thus, while allowing currencies to float, the tax would be likely to reduce short-term volatility. In addition, it would assist countries in retaining some degree of macroeconomic control over their own economies: "to preserve a local currency with residual monetary sovereignty, some friction in international financial institutions and markets needs to be retained. . . . Flows of capital to developing countries should preferably take the form of fixed direct investment or equity" (Tobin 1998: 7).

A Tobin Tax would also generate considerable revenue that could be used to relieve the most extreme poverty and encourage development. Even if it were substantially successful in reducing short-term currency speculation, it would still be likely to generate large sums, comparable in size to a GRD. Estimates vary greatly, but one recent proposal projects that a *very* small tax of 0.005 percent would generate between $10 and $15 billion each year (Kapoor 2004: 16). It is important to note that both the Tobin Tax and the GRD would work through, rather than replace, markets. A Tobin Tax does not peg currency prices at fixed levels; a GRD allows countries to determine the extent of their resource extraction. Both systems specify property rights in such a way that market institutions would be geared to help those who would otherwise be left behind. Neither of these proposals aims to arrest globalization, but rather to harness the power of markets in order to ensure that their benefits are more widely shared than they would be under a *laissez-faire* regime.

Certainly there would be practical difficulties with these proposals, but they are by no means insurmountable. When countries are united in their determination to achieve a goal, they adapt existing institutions or create new ones to achieve their purpose. We have already seen an example of this with the agreement on TRIMs, designed to facilitate multilateral agreements on financial liberalization. But an even more dramatic example was the inclusion of an agreement concerning trade-Related Intellectual Property (TRIPs) also concluded during the Uruguay Round of GATT negotiations in 1994. This agreement, in effect, made the WTO into an enforcer of international patents, trademarks, and trade secrets. Intellectual property rights allow a producer to hold a monopoly on the production of some good for a fixed period of time. Defenders argue that this spurs innovation and technology transfers, while detractors say that it limits competition and keeps prices high, including, significantly, the price of new drugs.[5] These competing interests in innovation and in access must be balanced very carefully. But this has little to do with facilitating trade in goods and services, the ostensible mandate of the WTO, and as one defender of the WTO puts it, it is at best a "difficult fit in the WTO system" (K. Jones 2004: 160; Bhagwati 2002: 75–6). It is a failure of political will, not any technical difficulties, that blocks the implementation of a Tobin Tax and GRD.

International labor and environmental standards have been a flashpoint for critics of globalization, especially since the protests at the 1999 meetings of the WTO in Seattle. I can only provide the briefest consideration of these issues. In the framework of global justice adopted here, labor and environmental standards become directly operative only when basic human rights are at stake. Beyond the protection of basic human rights, global justice does not require higher levels of protection. Higher standards are often important and valuable, and in many cases they are properly required by principles of domestic justice. But they are not a matter of global justice, and should not be subject to international enforcement. This becomes clear when we ask how these higher levels should be determined, and by whom. In the absence of a global state, the only answer can be that they should be set through the legitimate political institutions of different countries, both individually and through negotiated agreements. We can expect that countries will want to set these requirements at different levels for a variety of reasons. For example, countries may view their relationship to various parts of nature in different ways and be willing to make different levels of sacrifice in light of these conceptions. These differences may also reflect varying levels of economic development and willingness and ability to pay for environmental protection (Dasgupta et al. 1995: 19). Similar considerations apply to labor standards.

As an example illustrating the violation of basic human rights, consider that one recent study estimated that there are some 27 million people held against their will by their employers, the majority in debt bondage. They are, in other words, slaves (Bales 1999: 8–9). Legal ownership of another person is rarely asserted today, and in few countries is race the organizing concept of these modern forms of slavery (Bales 1999: 11, 80–120). Instead, in exchange for a monetary loan, people are put to work and are held against their wills through violence and threats of violence. Sometimes they are simply kidnapped. In 2002, the International Labor Organization (ILO) estimated that "at least 8.4 million girls and boys of all ages" fall into the category of the "unconditionally worst forms of child labour," which it defines as "slavery, trafficking, debt bondage and other forms of forced labour, recruitment of children for use in armed conflict, prostitution and pornography, and illicit activities" (International Labour Organization 2002: 17, 9). In cases such as these, the violations are so obvious and blatant that sophisticated conceptions of global justice seem beside the point. Again, it is largely a lack of political will that stands in the way of eliminating these horrifying practices.

As long as basic human rights are protected, however, countries should be able to decide for themselves, through their legitimate political institutions, how various trade-offs should be made. To repeat: this does not mean that any decision a country makes would be just, let alone beyond criticism. But if a country has a legitimate political structure, it should have the freedom to set its own priorities and requirements as long as it does not put its own legitimacy into question or impose excessive unchosen burdens on other societies.[6] Another country that disagrees with a particular decision should be free, of course, to pursue bilateral and multilateral agreements concerning environmental, labor, and other matters, in which the parties commit themselves to upholding standards above the minimal level required by global justice.

As an example of this process, consider a high-profile case that generated great hostility toward global trade organizations and globalization in general. In 1991, the United States sought to impose trade restrictions on tuna imported from Mexico that had been caught using a type of net that frequently resulted in the death of dolphins. A panel of the GATT issued a report that found that the US ban was in violation of trade rules and called for bilateral negotiations between the USA and Mexico to resolve the dispute. Mexico, engaged in negotiations over the North American Free Trade Agreement (NAFTA), chose not to pursue the matter further, and the report was never officially adopted by the GATT council. "In 1997, the United States ended its outright embargo on tuna caught using unacceptable fishing methods and focused instead on eco-labeling as part of an international dolphin-protection treaty signed with Mexico and other countries" (K. Jones 2004: 109).

This ruling is routinely described by environmentalists as an instance of a trade organization "overruling" or "striking down" US environmental law (Singer 2002: 58). This is not accurate. The WTO has no power to make (or unmake) law (and the GATT was even less powerful). As we saw above, the most it can do (beyond potentially shaming a country by ruling against it) is to authorize a country to impose its own retaliatory tariffs. The WTO cannot force a country to accept products that it objects to on environmental (or any other) grounds. It can, however, raise the cost of excluding such commodities. This is appropriate. If a country wants other countries to adopt a more demanding environmental standard than they would otherwise accept, it should be willing to pay a higher price to achieve it. It is important to remember that countries may reasonably make different decisions about which environmental standards are worth the cost. When a country imposes a tariff or embargo on another country because it wants it to adopt a more demanding standard, it raises the cost for the other country to maintain the weaker standard. If the WTO authorizes retaliatory tariffs, it shifts some of the costs back to the country that wants the more demanding standard. The USA, in demanding that Mexico use dolphin-safe nets – nets that Mexico may legitimately have decided were not worth the price – should have been prepared to pay the cost of this higher level of environmental protection. It could, for example, have offered to pay for the nets. It is worth emphasizing that it is almost always wealthy countries that seek to impose tougher environmental standards on poorer ones. As Bhagwati argues, "the rich and powerful countries that wish to propagate their moral preferences, whether widely held or idiosyncratic, should proceed to subsidize the PPMs [production and process methods] that they advocate . . . putting their own resources where they claim their moral preferences are" (Bhagwati 2004: 157–8). I want to stress once again that this is not an argument against higher environmental standards. Societies can and should impose appropriate protective measures on themselves through their legitimate political institutions and through negotiation with others. And if a country wants to encourage others to raise their standards beyond the levels that they would otherwise accept, it should be willing to enter negotiations to pay for part of the cost of doing so.

It is sometimes objected that in a context of global markets, if different countries have different environmental and labor standards, there will be a "race to the bottom." The thought is that countries with lower environmental and labor standards would have a competitive advantage over those with higher standards, since companies could operate at a lower cost in the former. Thus, those with higher standards would face financial pressure to lower theirs in order to compete. Although such an outcome is theoretically possible, the evidence indicates that this has not happened with respect to either environmental or labor standards. The competitive advantages that might be gained from lower standards appear to be swamped by other considerations. The available evidence suggests that

> an environmental "race to the bottom" appears extremely unlikely. In fact, the converse appears to occur as "the bottom" rises with economic growth. The poorest societies persistently improve their environmental quality as investment increases employment and income. . . . Communities in developing countries are neither passive agents nor focused exclusively on material gain. Empowered with good information about the benefits and costs of environmental protection, they will act to protect their own interests. As their income and education levels improve, they will control pollution more strictly. (Wheeler 2002: 11, 13; cf. Copeland and Taylor 2003; Antweiler et al. 2001; Grether and de Melo 2003)

Similarly, I know of no evidence that countries with relaxed labor regulations (for example, health and safety requirements) have a statistically significant competitive advantage over those with tight regulations. On the contrary, there is some evidence that there is "a mutually supportive relationship between successfully sustained trade reforms and improvements in association and bargaining rights" (Organization for Economic Cooperation and Development 1996: 112). There seems to be no more a race to the bottom with respect to labor regulations than there is with respect to environmental regulations. There is, however, some evidence that differences in prevailing wage rates might induce companies to move or outsource to low-wage countries. Often, however, this tendency is greatly overstated. It is important to remember that a competitive advantage in one area, such as lower prevailing wage rates, is often outweighed by disadvantages in other areas, such as productivity and infrastructure. In summary, as one author from the ILO writes: "There is no clear evidence that globalization has caused a lowering of labour standards in industrialized countries. . . . If trade with low-wage countries has had only a limited impact on employment and wages in the industrialized countries [as the evidence suggests], then it must follow that it could not have exerted any downward pressure on labour standards either" (Lee 1997: 182–3).

While there seems to be little evidence of a race to the bottom, increased competition does generate greater insecurity. This is true for both wealthy and poor countries. Some claim that states have become powerless and irrelevant in the face of global markets. While it is true that many countries have become increasingly subject to forces beyond their control, there is a greater and greater need for states to respond appropriately concerning the factors that they *can* control. These functions include assisting citizens in preparing to compete in global markets – for example, through investment in infrastructure and education and training – and by cushioning the downsides of competition, both for individuals who lose out as well as for the economy as a whole (Weiss 1998; J. R. Mandle 2003). As Kitching argues:

> It is important that the world's advanced capitalist states act . . . to reduce the levels of anxiety of their populations about the globalization process by putting in place *social policies* that make these anxieties and the insecurities easier to cope with. I have in mind large investments in education, training, and retraining programs that can make their working populations as change-adaptive as it is possible for them to be. But I also have in mind the maintenance of good-quality mass access to health, social security, and other programs. (Kitching 2001: 290)

When a country has a legitimate political structure, it can use these institutions to make and impose on itself decisions concerning labor and environmental laws, as well as what kinds of economic strategies to pursue and what policies to protect its citizens from the insecurities associated with those policies.

Poor countries especially need assistance in order to cushion the disruptions associated with market integration. Consider just a single example. In 1999, the WTO ruled against the preferential scheme that some European countries showed toward bananas imported from the West Indies. Bhagwati comments that "while such a finding was absolutely correct in law, its impact was to leave these small and poor

Caribbean nations with an estimated loss in their national incomes of up to 15 percent!" (Bhagwati 2004: 235). Upon investigation, Bhagwati was shocked to find that the World Bank had no "program of special aid to compensate and otherwise assist these countries facing huge losses. While the aid sums would be large for these small countries, they would be negligible as a fraction of what the World Bank spends and disburses" (p. 235). In general, Bhagwati argues, "the Bank should automatically trigger support when the WTO's Dispute Settlement Mechanism brings a significant loss of income and attending adjustment problem for producers in poor countries who have lost market access" (pp. 235–6; cf. J. R. Mandle 2003: 126–7). Despite being arguably the leading defender of free trade, Bhagwati is no market fundamentalist. He emphasizes the need for institutional policies at both the state level and the global level, to ensure that the benefits of globalization are equitably distributed (Bhagwati 2004: 239).

At the limit, a country could decide to forgo any further growth or trade with other countries. No country has made such an extreme choice, but smaller sacrifices in growth are made all the time, in order to pursue other goals they deem to be valuable. Since countries have overwhelmingly opted to pursue growth through expanded trade, it is hard to see what objections there could be to the existence of an institutional structure to facilitate and coordinate these shared goals. There is, however, plenty of room to criticize the institutions that currently manage globalization. The IMF and the World Bank too often pursue a market-fundamentalist agenda that destabilizes economies. None is transparent enough (Woods 2001; Stiglitz 2003). The WTO has extended itself beyond its core mission of facilitating trade in goods and services and has become an enforcer of intellectual property, and it has been too hesitant to pressure wealthy countries to reduce their agricultural and textile subsidies and tariffs. These failures, of course, reflect the wishes of the more powerful countries. On the other hand, there is little doubt that powerful countries are currently *less* able to impose their wills on others than they would be if these global institutions did not exist. Powerful countries still shape the rules and violate them when they want to, but they cannot do this with the kind of impunity that they would enjoy without these institutions. In March 2002, for example, the US unilaterally imposed a 30 percent tariff on imported steel. By some estimates, the Brazilian steel industry stood to lose up to $1 billion, and 5,000 jobs were in jeopardy (Oxfam 2002a). Eventually, the WTO ruled against the USA, and it lifted the tariffs in December 2003. Serious damage was done, but in the absence of a WTO, such episodes would be the rule and not the exception, since there would be far less pressure on rich countries to back down from such unilateral impositions.

Another set of problems associated with our current global institutional structure is related to the unbalanced way in which they have developed. Although there are global institutions devoted to protecting human rights and the environment, they simply do not have anything like the authority that those devoted to the global economy currently enjoy. It is natural that supporters of these other causes would want the existing powerful institutions to expand their areas of concern to encompass these additional concerns. This is probably a mistake. Quite simply, the WTO would be a poor monitor and enforcer of human rights and environmental agreements. It would probably be better to expand and empower the institutions dedicated to these causes, such as the International Labour Organization (ILO) and the United Nations Commission on Human Rights, and to create a Global Environmental Organization (GEO) that could coordinate and facilitate bilateral and multilateral environmental agreements (Runge 2001). To be sure, it would not be easy to create institutions powerful enough to enforce such agreements, but there is no reason to think that the existing economic institutions will *ever* be effective at pursuing these goals (Dommen 2002; K. Jones 2004; Esty 1993).

The changes I have mentioned, such as agreeing to a GRD, implementing a Tobin Tax, making the World Bank, the IMF, and the WTO more open, strengthening the ILO, and creating a GEO, would reorient the process of globalization so that it would work to everyone's advantage more fairly. But they would not challenge the underlying logic of expanding markets across borders, and for some critics of globalization, this is exactly the problem. While reluctantly conceding that expanded markets would perhaps increase aggregate wealth and that with proper institutional reforms this increase could help relieve poverty, these critics argue that the non-economic costs are simply too high. Many such critics focus on the *cultural* implications of globalization. The central organizing concept of this critique is that globalization results in the "homogenization" of culture. The fear is of a "global mono-culture" in which "Every place is becoming more and more like every other place" (International Forum on Globalization 2002: 23; cf. Barnet and Cavanagh 1996). Benjamin Barber, in a book entitled *Jihad vs. McWorld*, argues that globalization's "homogenization is likely to establish a macropeace that favors the triumph of commerce and its markets" (Barber 1996: 20). Barber grants that globalization may increase wealth and the prospects for peace, but these gains pale in comparison to the more serious and subtle corruption associated with markets: "McWorld's denizens are consumers and clients whose freedom consists of the right to buy in markets they cannot control and whose identity is imposed on them by a consumerism they scarcely notice" (p. 223).

There can be no doubt that the forces of globalization result in dramatic changes to cultures and ways of life, but it is not obvious that these changes should be characterized as homogenization and a loss of diversity. Critics often lament the alleged loss of regionally specific cuisine, architecture, and music, for example. Even a popular defender of globalization such as Thomas Friedman worries about this prospect: "Everywhere will start to look like everywhere else. . . . Touring the world will become like going to the zoo and seeing the same animal in every cage – a stuffed animal" (Friedman 1999: 221–2). The loss of regional specificity is, however, compatible with a different sense of diversity. If cultures and practices are not limited by geography and can increasingly spread across borders, different places may look more and more alike, but they will do so by offering *more* opportunities to individuals who can experience and participate in cultural forms previously unavailable to them. Such changes would involve a loss in diversity only from the perspective of wealthy tourists, who would be less able to experience exotic and unfamiliar cultures and locations. For most people it would involve a significant gain. As Tyler Cowen observes, "Cross-cultural exchange tends to favor diversity within society, but to disfavor diversity across societies" (Cowen 2002: 15).

Almost by definition, the process of globalization dramatically increases the frequency of interaction among previously isolated cultures. Without a doubt, this has led to a significant increase in the cultural diversity within societies. As Cowen points out, "individuals are liberated from the *tyranny of place* more than ever before. ... This change represents one of the most significant increases in freedom in human history" (Cowen 2002: 5; cf. 129). Such a process may result in some loss of diversity *among* societies, although I believe that critics exaggerate the extent to which this has happened. Furthermore, it is important to recognize that some forms of homogenization are in no way regrettable. It would be an unambiguous good to have a world in which basic human rights were universally respected. The process of economic development inevitably influences more than just production methods. As individuals move out of poverty, some practices are left behind with few if any regrets. In other cases, however, there is genuine loss.

What cultural critics of globalization *really* object to, I suggest, is the substantive effects that they believe markets have on culture. As Cowen argues, "much of the skepticism about cross-cultural exchange has nothing to do with diversity per se. Most critics of contemporary culture dislike particular trends, often those associated with modernity or commercialism more generally" (Cowen 2002: 17; cf. 132–5). Cultural critics of globalization miss the mark when they condemn homogenization, but they can reasonably raise the question of whether the dramatic changes in culture that globalization brings about are good or bad – whether they constitute cultural progress and improvement or degeneration and loss. Some changes open up new and productive areas of creativity, while others wash away valuable traditions in a wave of trendy ephemera.

From the point of view of justice, the crucial fact is that there is almost always reasonable disagreement about whether a particular change is good or bad. For almost any prospective change, some people will enthusiastically embrace the new, while others will adhere to the old. Sometimes these disputes are cast in terms of what is the true or authentic interpretation of a practice and what is an external corruption. It certainly cannot be the case that justice prohibits all changes

to cultures, or even those changes that are prompted or insti-
gated by external developments. That would make cultures
into museum pieces, whereas cultures are kept vital by trans-
forming traditions, incorporating formerly foreign elements,
and adapting to new circumstances. As Jeremy Waldron
observes, to deny a culture the ability to incorporate new
elements and re-interpret old elements in response to new
pressures and opportunities is to deny it "what many would
regard as its most fascinating feature: its ability to generate *a
history*" (Waldron 1992: 788). Still, there is no rule by which
to determine whether a proposed change is good or bad.
When confronted with the forces of globalization, societies
must decide whether to take steps to preserve their traditional
ways of life against the modernizing tendencies of market
forces. Defenders of traditional practices may *rightly* argue
that without special subsidies, they will not be able to compete
and will be forced to abandon their traditional ways of life.
Society, they claim, should sacrifice other goals and interests
to preserve these traditions. Others may argue in reply that
although this involves a genuine loss, preserving traditional
practices would involve sacrificing other creative opportunities of greater value. "No society can include within itself all
forms of life . . . there is no social world without loss: that is,
no social world that does not exclude some ways of life that
realize in special ways certain fundamental values" (Rawls
1996: 197). Choices must be made, because values conflict.

In such cases, when basic rights are not at stake, at the level
of global justice we must adopt a procedural perspective.
What matters from the point of view of global justice is not a
substantive judgment about whether a practice constitutes
progress or decline, but that legitimate political institutions be
in place to allow a society to make a collective decision about
how to handle such disputes. Through its legitimate political
institutions, a society might decide to adopt a policy of
"benign neglect," in which it does not use state power deliberately to promote or hinder any particular cultural practice
(Brighouse 1998). Other options, such as subsidizing or officially recognizing or otherwise encouraging certain practices,
are consistent with global justice as well (Kymlicka 1995).
What is not acceptable, of course, is attempting to influence
a cultural practice in a way that violates basic human rights.

In this context, the human rights most likely to be implicated are liberty of conscience and freedom of expression. For example, it would be unjust to attempt to preserve a traditional practice by prohibiting apostasy or by outlawing a certain language.

The point is not that political institutions are necessarily good judges concerning cultural matters. The decisions they make may not accurately reflect the true value of a cultural practice. Sometimes a society may make a tragic decision that it comes to regret when it fails to protect some valuable practice. But there seems to be no other option beyond letting people make such judgments for themselves through their legitimate political institutions. This account is neither a defense of political intervention into cultural matters nor a defense of pure market relations in influencing cultural production. Nor do I claim that the decisions made by legitimate political institutions will always be just according to some specific conception of *domestic* justice.[7] However, as long as they do not involve the violation of basic human rights, and as long as legitimate political institutions are in place to make such collective decisions, they will be acceptable from the point of view of global justice. Just as legitimate societies may make their own decisions about environmental and social welfare policies, so too they may make their own decisions about cultural policies.

The picture of a just global order that I have presented is one in which basic human rights are protected primarily by legitimate states. The primary responsibility for securing and protecting basic human rights falls on the political structure of a society, and thus on one's fellow citizens, who act as a corporate body through these structures. When these institutions fail to protect, or even violate, basic human rights, the weight of the duties shifts in a more cosmopolitan direction. Duties of global justice are owed across borders, even if people do not share political institutions, precisely because all people are entitled to human rights, and everyone – not only fellow citizens – is bound to respect them. Although there may be crises that call for direct humanitarian intervention or assistance, the long-term goal is to establish legitimate political structures that allow a society to secure its own basic rights. From this baseline, a country can freely make collective decisions concerning how it will pursue its various goals, including setting labor and environmental standards and shaping its cultural activities, as well as pursuing mutually advantageous interactions with others.

This is not the world that we currently live in; nor is it one that we have ever had. But for the first time, it is arguably possible to create such a world. A failure to move toward it is our collective failure, not attributable to limitations beyond human control. The account that I have presented is what Rawls calls a "realistic utopia" (in fact, it is close to the one that Rawls himself advocates) (Rawls 1999b: 5–6, 11–12). A presentation of a realistic utopia

> establishes that such a world can exist somewhere and at some time, but not that it must be, or will be. . . . The possibility is not a mere logical possibility, but one that connects with the deep tendencies and inclination of the social world. For so long as we believe for good reasons that a self-sustaining and reasonably just political and social order both at home and abroad is possible, we can reasonably hope that we or others will someday, somewhere, achieve it; and we can then do something toward this achievement. This alone, quite apart from our success or failure, suffices to banish the dangers of resignation and cynicism. By showing how the social world may realize the features of a realistic utopia, political philosophy provides a long-term goal of political endeavor, and in working toward it gives meaning to what we can do today. (Rawls 1999b: 127–8)

On the one hand, in order to serve as a standard of evaluation from which to guide reform, such an account cannot be confined to existing institutions and practices. It must project a model of what a just order could look like if things went well. On the other hand, it must provide a workable conception that could be put into practice and that does not ignore deep features of the human condition such as the diversity of conflicting values and comprehensive doctrines.

There is an additional condition that Rawls does not mention but that I believe is crucial in constructing a realistic utopia.[8] It is important to identify a path from our present situation to a just order that does not depend on first making things dramatically worse. When we find injustice all around us, there is nothing wrong in hoping that people will recoil and pursue the cause of justice. However, if progress toward justice is not forthcoming, its advocates must not be put in the position in which they hope for things to get worse, in order to trigger a desired backlash. Such a position is both morally bankrupt and politically suicidal. We must find a path toward justice that does not depend on a backlash against still greater injustice, but one that steers existing forces in a positive direction. The point of creating such scenarios is not that they are inevitable, or even likely, but only that they are, as Nielsen puts it, "in the realm of *empirically reasonable political possibilities*" (Nielsen 2003: 270).

Globalization has greatly expanded the interaction among people across borders. To be sure, their primary interaction is through trade, and the relationships developed there are limited. However, it is important not to be naïve about the attitudes that existed before the recent dramatic expansion of global market relations. Historically, relations among societies have often been less than admirable. At best, they were frequently based on ignorance and indifference. At worst, there was a violent hostility toward foreigners and unfamiliar ways of life. When people are indifferent or hostile toward one another, establishing market interactions may be an important first step in creating relations of respect and toleration and the possible discovery or creation of a deeper consensus. As Rawls observes,

> relations of affinity are not a fixed thing, but may continually grow stronger over time as peoples come to work together in cooperative institutions they have developed. It is characteristic of liberal and decent peoples that they seek a world in which all peoples have a well-ordered [legitimate] regime. At first we may suppose this aim is moved by each people's *self-interest*, for such regimes are not dangerous but peaceful and cooperative. Yet as cooperation between peoples proceeds apace they may come to care about each other, and affinity between them becomes stronger. Hence, they are no longer moved simply by self-interest but by mutual concern for each other's way of life and culture, and they become willing to make sacrifices for each other. This mutual caring is the outcome of their fruitful cooperative efforts and common experiences over a considerable period of time.

The relatively narrow circle of mutually caring peoples in the world today may expand over time and must never be viewed as fixed. (Rawls 1999b: 112–13)

When one keeps in mind the diversity of the world's cultures, practices, and values, and the history of indifference and hostility across borders, it seems that the process of globalization might eventually lead to greater humanizing tendencies. I would not venture to guess whether we are moving toward or away from this goal, but this is at least a possible path in the direction of global justice. If, as I have argued, such a path is possible but not inevitable, then our job is not simply to moralize, but to help steer us all onto this path.

Notes

Chapter 1 Ethical Theory

1 We are considering what is sometimes called "agent's group relativism," as opposed to "appraiser's group relativism" (Lyons 1976: 109–11).

Chapter 2 Justice

1 It is too much to demand that these principles be accepted by everyone. Rather, what is required is that they be acceptable to all *reasonable* people. How this limit is drawn is a difficult matter. The question (at the methodological level) is analogous to, but distinct from, the substantive question of who to tolerate (J. Mandle 1999).
2 Notice that the idea of a political conception of justice does not place a restriction on offering justifications based on specific comprehensive ethical or religious doctrines. It says that if they are presented, there must *also* be justifications offered that could be accepted by all reasonable people (Rawls 1999b: 152–6).
3 The first three of these, together with justice, are Aristotle's four cardinal virtues.

Chapter 3 Realism, Nationalism, and Cosmopolitanism

1 Thucydides himself, in addition to the views that he attributes to the Athenians, is also frequently regarded as a political realist. However, see Ahrensdorf 1997.

2 Realists are very slippery in their use of these crucial terms. Sometimes, "power" is understood so inclusively that virtually everything a country does is by definition an exercise in power. Morgenthau officially defines power simply as "man's control over the minds and actions of other men," and he states that it "derives from three sources: the expectation of benefits, the fear of disadvantages, the respect or love for men or institutions" (Morgenthau and Thompson 1985: 32). Other times, however, his focus is much narrower, distinguishing it from the economic, financial, or military goals that a country might pursue (p.36). For other realists, such as John Mearsheimer, power simply means military power together with "the socio-economic ingredients that go into building military power" (Mearsheimer 2001: 55; cf. Waltz 1979 and Keohane and Nye 2001: 20). With an expansive interpretation, the realist claim that nations ought to pursue power becomes trivial, and realism's "tough mindedness" evaporates as a nation is said to be pursuing power whether it aims to expand economic trade, achieve cultural hegemony, attain military dominance, or promote respect for basic human rights. With a narrow interpretation, the explanatory adequacy of realism is greatly diminished, and the realist owes us an account of why all other goals should be subordinated to this single end.

3 Note that this account does not prejudge the proper criteria for membership in a particular nation. For example, it might be a controversial matter who is to count as a Serbian or a Zimbabwean or an Israeli. This account also allows these criteria to change over time.

4 Miller sometimes emphasizes political structures rather than national identity, e.g. D. Miller 1998a: 179. But more typically, he emphasizes the subjective identification that I have emphasized.

Chapter 4 Human Rights

1 Technically, there is a contrast between enjoying the *content* of a right and enjoying the right itself – that is, enjoying the social protection of the content. There are two corresponding senses in

which a right might be violated: when the content of the right is actually denied, and when a society fails to provide adequate protection for it against standard threats. As we will see below, it is possible for a right to be violated in one sense but not in the other. In most cases, however, we will assume that a violation involves the content being denied because of inadequate social protections.

2 Rawls's idea of an overlapping consensus concerns agreement on a full conception of justice, not simply human rights (Rawls 1996: 133–72).

3 This is more expansive than Rawls's understanding of liberty of conscience (cf. Beitz 2004: 203).

Chapter 5 Challenges to Human Rights

1 However, even Cranston recognizes that some rights require positive action and not only protection from the government, since he immediately goes on to discuss the right to a trial by jury.

2 The charge of arrogance seems to lie behind the attitude of some realists, including George Kennan: "this whole tendency to see ourselves as the center of political enlightenment and as teachers to a great part of the rest of the world strikes me as unthought-through, vainglorious, and undesirable" (quoted in Ullman 1999: 6).

3 For the grim list of particulars, see Rummel 1994 and Glover 1999.

4 The paragraph concludes by stating that "this principle shall not prejudice the application of enforcement measures under Chapter VII." Chapter VII concerns the ability of the Security Council to authorize the use of force when it finds a "threat to the peace, breach of the peace, or act of aggression." A persistent source of controversy concerns whether these clauses imply an international dimension.

5 The convention went into effect in 1951. Although an original signatory, the USA only ratified the Convention in 1988. And it did so with a reservation that, in effect, gutted its binding character by stating that "the specific consent of the United States is required in each case [to which the US is a party]" before the case may be submitted to the International Court of Justice.

6 The USA has been a conspicuous outlier on ratification of international human rights covenants. In addition to rejecting the 1995 creation of the International Criminal Court, it ratified the International Covenant on Civil and Political Rights only in 1992, "and then only with a brace of reservations to ensure it would

have little or no domestic effect" (Glendon 2001: 213). And although President Carter signed the Covenant on Economic, Social, and Cultural Rights in 1976, it has not been ratified – indeed, it has never even been considered by the Senate. There are numerous other examples of international covenants never signed or ratified by the USA, including the 1951 Convention on the Status of Refugees, 1969 Inter-American Convention on Human Rights, the 1979 Covenant on Women's Rights, the 1989 Convention on the Rights of the Child, and the 1997 Convention on Landmines.

7 Even the 1993 Bangkok declaration issued by Asian countries prior to the Vienna conference, while emphasizing "the significance of national and regional particularities and various historical, cultural and religious backgrounds," also reaffirmed the UDHR and stressed "the universality, objectivity and non-selectivity of all human rights . . . and that no violation of human rights can be justified" (World Conference on Human Rights 1993).

Chapter 6   Political Legitimacy

1 This discussion draws on J. Mandle 2005.
2 Rawls leaves it an open question whether any actual societies fall into this category (Rawls 1999b: 75, n. 16).
3 To avoid confusion, I should note immediately that I am using "legitimate" in a normative sense. Many social scientists use it merely to indicate *de facto* support for a regime, regardless of its moral status. On my account, such support is a necessary but not sufficient condition for legitimacy.
4 In addition to specifying purely procedural elements, many constitutions impose substantive constraints on law through a Bill of Rights.
5 As the 2000 presidential election, in which Al Gore received more than 500,000 more popular votes than George W. Bush, reminds us, this is not merely a theoretical point (cf. Ackerman 2002; Laden 2002).
6 If there is more than one possible institutional mechanism to make legitimate law, a society needs to make a kind of second-order collective decision about which structure to use. Legitimacy requires, therefore, that the procedure itself have widespread support.
7 Allen Buchanan points out that there is an additional requirement: that it has not usurped power from a previous legitimate

regime. We can ignore this here, but it is often relevant in discussion of secession (Buchanan 2004: 275–6).

8 Rawls also suggests that it would be inappropriate to offer incentives to help a decent hierarchical society become more just (according to liberal principles) (Rawls 1999b: 84–5). It is possible that such incentives would work as a subtle form of coercion, if there is an implicit threat to withhold what is owed as a matter of justice. But if this is avoided, I see no reason in principle why a liberal society should not be allowed, if it chooses, to assist a decent hierarchical society to become more just (cf. Freeman 2002: 60, n. 84).

9 To simplify, I here leave aside the cases of refugees, resident aliens, and visitors. Generally speaking, the problem of refugees should be addressed in the context of duties to people who lack a legitimate political order. The fact that visitors temporarily subject themselves voluntarily to the laws of a foreign territory does not seem to raise any fundamental questions of justice. But resident aliens, it seems, have a fairly strong claim to participate in at least some of the political decisions of their host country.

10 There is little consensus concerning whether granting some degree of autonomy to nationalist groups tends to increase or decrease their calls for secession. Kymlicka, for example, worries that "If limited autonomy is granted to a national minority, this may simply fuel the ambitions of nationalist leaders, who may be satisfied with nothing short of their own nation-state. Democratic multination states which recognize self-government rights are, it appears, inherently unstable for this reason" (Kymlicka 1996: 122). There is, however, some evidence that suggests that "whereas federation stimulates nationalist political mobilization, it decreases nationalist violence" (Hechter 2000b: 14–15; cf. Hechter 2000a; Lustick et al. 2004).

11 Walzer is summarizing John Stuart Mill's argument, but it is clear that he endorses it.

12 This suggests that Moellendorf's first criterion is too weak. Given the near certainty that the use of military force will produce at least some – and often very many – civilian casualties, there should be a considerably higher likelihood of success than of failure.

Chapter 7   Poverty and Development

1 Reddy and Pogge (2003) argue that the $1 per day (PPP) standard is flawed and results in an under-assessment of the extent of extreme poverty. Nonetheless, it remains the standard measure.

2 In 1993, the base year from which the $1 per day measure is cal-
culated, the US government set the poverty line for an individual
at $7,363. In 2003, it was $9,393 (United States Census Bureau
2004).

3 Although the US Census Bureau collects data on the number of
people living below the poverty level, it is difficult to get reliable
data about more extreme poverty in the USA. A 1999 study
published by the US Department of Housing and Urban
Development, relying on data from 1996, found that in a 30-day
period, the median income among homeless clients was $300,
and 45 percent reported receiving "some type of means-tested
government assistance," including food stamps (Interagency
Council on Homelessness 1999: 5–1; cf. 5–4, table 5.1). I in no
way mean to imply that these provisions for homeless people are
generous or even adequate. But they are far above the international $2 per day level that we are discussing.

4 Actually, some 30 million people out of a population of 75
million were forced from their homes – the nine million figure is
approximately the number who crossed the border into India.
The eventual death toll from war and famine has been estimated
as high as three million, but is probably around half of that. The
three million figure likely derives from President Yahya Kahn of
Pakistan's claim, "Kill three million of them and the rest will eat
out of our hands" (Rummel 1994: 315–37; cf. Payne 1973).

5 One feature that makes it unsuitable to serve as an account of
justice is its rejection of the reasonable pluralism of values. Its
dogmatism on this point may be hidden by its subjective account
of values, relying on pleasure or satisfaction of preferences, for
example. But this subjectivism is itself something that people
may reasonably reject (J. Mandle 2000: 147–51).

6 The following discussion draws on J. Mandle 2003.

7 To be sure, such subjective identification may be an important
source of additional moral obligations, but this does not mean
that they can ground obligations of justice (cf. Caney 1999:
129–30).

8 Blake emphasizes that there are other forms of international
coercion, but he argues that these do not give rise to the same
kinds of egalitarian concerns that the coercive imposition of a
legal order does.

9 Other factors include the historical legacy of colonialism, the
persistence of bribery, and the specific terms of trade, negotiated
through the WTO. We will discuss the last of these in chapter 8.

10 Pogge contrasts this process to the case of a thief selling stolen
property to a "fence." Although the fence may have possession,

he is not the owner of the property. In particular, the state would be justified not in protecting his possession but in returning the property to its rightful owner.

11 Pogge has defended a global egalitarian principle of distributive justice in the past and continues to argue that Rawls's rejection of such a principle is ungrounded (Pogge 2002: 104–8). However, in his recent work, he noticeably avoids arguing directly in favor of a global egalitarian standard. Compare Pogge 1994: 196 and Pogge 2002: 36, 51, 96.

12 When the authors examined the effects on income inequality of various pro-growth policies, they also found "little evidence that these policies and institutions have systematic effects on the share of income accruing to the poorest quintile" (Dollar and Kraay 2002: 196).

13 Pogge makes several concrete proposals, only one of which we will discuss. Some of his other proposals include suggestions concerning the constitution of fledgling democracies and mechanisms for the withdrawal of support for illegitimate regimes (Pogge 2002: ch. 6; cf. Buchanan 2004: 278, 284).

14 This figure was endorsed by the UN General Assembly in 1970. See United Nations 1970: 146, box 8.2.

15 Between 1948 and 1951, the US GDP averaged $283 billion per year. At approximately $4.3 billion per year, the US spent around 1.52 percent of its GDP on the Marshall Plan. Data on GNP from United States Department of Commerce 1952: 253.

Chapter 8   Globalization

1 Through the 1960s and 1970s, and especially following the appointment of Robert McNamara as the bank's president in 1968, the World Bank shifted its focus to addressing poverty through providing assistance to development projects in poor countries.

2 Although it is often presented as aimed at saving small family farms, "nearly 70 percent of the subsidies go to the top 10 percent of agricultural producers."

3 Foreign direct investment (FDI) occurs when a corporation invests in and acquires control of real productive capital in a foreign country. This may involve either acquisition of existing assets or so-called Greenfield investment in which new facilities are created. Portfolio investment involves a transfer of ownership in existing capital, but not managerial control. Both FDI and portfolio investment need to be distinguished from currency

speculation in which there is no transfer of underlying productive capital. Both portfolio investment and currency speculation are far more volatile than FDI.

4 The following draws on J. Mandle 2000a.

5 Critics include Oxfam 2002b: ch. 8; defenders include the World Intellectual Property Organization (WIPO).

6 Global warming seems to be a case in which the major polluters are imposing significant unchosen burdens on other countries (Singer 2002: ch. 2; Gardiner 2004).

7 We cannot consider here what principles of *domestic* justice are appropriate to govern the relationship between a society and a cultural minority. I simply note that the account I have given of legitimacy is compatible with various forms of confederation and representation of national and cultural minorities. The literature on the relationship between principles of domestic justice and culture has grown rapidly in the last decade, following the pioneering work of Will Kymlicka. See e.g. Kymlicka 1995; Tomasi 1995; Waldron 1992; Barry 2001; Carens 2000; Benhabib 2002.

8 This and the following paragraph draw on J. Mandle, forthcoming.

References

Ackerman, B. (ed.) 2002: *Bush v. Gore: The Question of Legitimacy.* New Haven: Yale University Press.

Ahrensdorf, P. J. 1997: Thucydides' Realistic Critique of Realism. *Polity*, 30 (2), 231–65.

Alesina, A. and Dollar, D. 2000: Who Gives Foreign Aid to Whom and Why? *Journal of Economic Growth*, 5 (1), 33–63.

Amnesty International 2000: NATO/Federal Republic of Yugoslavia, "Collateral Damage" or Unlawful Killings? <http://www.amnesty.org/ailib/intcam/kosovo/docs/nato_all.pdf>

Anderson, B. 1991: *Imagined Communities: Reflections on the Origin and Spread of Nationalism*, rev. ed. New York: Verso.

An-Na'Im, A. A. 1992: Conclusion. In A. A. An-Na'Im (ed.), *Human Rights in Cross-Cultural Perspectives: A Quest for Consensus*, Philadelphia: University of Pennsylvania Press, 427–35.

Antweiler, W., Copeland, B. R. and Taylor, M. S. 2001: Is Free Trade Good for the Environment? *American Economic Review*, 91 (4), 877–908.

Baker, D., Epstein, G. and Pollin, R. 1998: Introduction. In D. Baker, G. Epstein, and R. Pollin (eds), *Globalization and Progressive Economic Policy*, New York: Cambridge University Press, 1–34.

Bales, K. 1999: *Disposable People: New Slavery in the Global Economy.* Berkeley: University of California Press.

Barber, B. R. 1996: *Jihad vs. McWorld: How Globalism and Tribalism Are Reshaping the World.* New York: Ballantine Books.

Bardhan, P. 1993: Symposium on Democracy and Development. *Journal of Economic Perspectives*, 7 (3), 45–9.

Barnet, R. and Cavanagh, J. 1996: Homogenization of Global Culture. In J. Mander and E. Goldsmith (eds), *The Case against the Global*

Economy: And for a Turn toward the Local, San Francisco: Sierra Club Books, 71–7.

Baron, H. 1987: *The Consent Theory of Political Obligation*. New York: Croom Helm.

Barry, B. 2001: *Culture and Equality: An Egalitarian Critique of Multiculturalism*. Cambridge, Mass.: Harvard University Press.

Bedau, H. A. 1979: Human Rights and Foreign Assistance Programs. In P. G. Brown and D. MacLean (eds), *Human Rights and U.S. Foreign Policy: Principles and Applications*, Lexington, Mass.: Lexington Books, 29–44.

Beitz, C. R. 1999: *Political Theory and International Relations*, 2nd edn. Princeton: Princeton University Press.

Beitz, C. R. 2004: Human Rights and the Law of Peoples. In D. K. Chatterjee (ed.), *The Ethics of Assistance: Morality and the Distant Needy*, New York: Cambridge University Press, 193–214.

Bell, D. A. 1996: The East Asian Challenge to Human Rights: Reflections on an East–West Dialogue. *Human Rights Quarterly*, 18 (3), 641–67.

Bell, D. A. 2000: *East Meets West: Human Rights and Democracy in East Asia*. Princeton: Princeton University Press.

Benedict, R. 2001: Anthropology and the Abnormal. In P. K. Moser and T. L. Carson (eds), *Moral Relativism: A Reader*, New York: Oxford University Press, 80–9.

Benhabib, S. 2002: *The Claims of Culture: Equality and Diversity in the Global Era*. Princeton: Princeton University Press.

Bernstein, A. unpublished: "A Cosmopolitan Law of Peoples."

Beversluis, E. H. 1989: On Shunning Undesirable Regimes: Ethics and Economic Sanctions. *Public Affairs Quarterly*, 3 (2), 15–26.

Bhagwati, J. 1998: The Capital Myth: The Difference between Trade in Widgets and Dollars. *Foreign Affairs*, 77 (3), 7–12.

Bhagwati, J. 2002: *Free Trade Today*. Princeton: Princeton University Press.

Bhagwati, J. 2004: *In Defense of Globalization*. New York: Oxford University Press.

Blake, M. 2001: Distributive Justice, State Coercion, and Autonomy. *Philosophy and Public Affairs*, 30 (3), 257–96.

Boxill, B. R. 1987: Global Equality of Opportunity and National Integrity. *Social Philosophy and Policy*, 5, 143–68.

Brandt, R. B. 1972: Utilitarianism and War. *Philosophy and Public Affairs*, 1 (2), 145–65.

Brighouse, H. 1998: Against Nationalism. In J. Couture, K. Nielsen, and M. Seymour (eds), *Rethinking Nationalism*, Canadian Journal of Philosophy suppl. vol. 22 (1996), Calgary, Alberta: University of Calgary Press, 365–405.

Buchanan, A. 1997: Theories of Secession. *Philosophy and Public Affairs*, 26 (1), 31–61.

Buchanan, A. 1998: What's So Special about Nations? In J. Couture, K. Nielsen, and M. Seymour (eds), *Rethinking Nationalism*, Canadian Journal of Philosophy suppl. vol. 22 (1996), Calgary, Alberta: University of Calgary Press, 283–309.

Buchanan, A. 2004: *Justice, Legitimacy, and Self-Determination: Moral Foundations for International Law.* New York: Oxford University Press.

Calhoun, C. 1997: *Nationalism.* Minneapolis: University of Minnesota Press.

Caney, S. 1999: Nationality, Distributive Justice and the Use of Force. *Journal of Applied Philosophy*, 16 (2), 123–38.

Caney, S. 2001: Cosmopolitan Justice and Equalizing Opportunities. *Metaphilosophy*, 32 (1/2), 113–34.

Carens, J. H. 1995: Aliens and Citizens: The Case for Open Borders. In W. Kymlicka (ed.), *The Rights of Minority Cultures*, New York: Oxford University Press, 331–49.

Carens, J. H. 2000: *Culture, Citizenship, and Community: A Contextual Exploration of Justice as Evenhandedness.* New York: Oxford University Press.

Chen, S. and Ravallion, M. 2004: *How Have the World's Poorest Fared since the Early 1980s?* World Bank Policy Research Working Paper 3341. <http://econ.worldbank.org/files/36297_wps3341.pdf>

Chomsky, N. 1999: *The New Military Humanism: Lessons from Kosovo.* Monroe, Me.: Common Courage Press.

Christie, K. 1995: Regime Security and Human Rights in Southeast Asia. *Political Studies*, 43 (special issue), 204–18.

Coady, C. A. J. 2003: War for Humanity: A Critique. In D. K. Chatterjee and D. E. Scheid (eds), *Ethics and Foreign Intervention*, New York: Cambridge University Press, 274–95.

Cohen, J. 1986: Review of *Spheres of Justice*, by Michael Walzer. *Journal of Philosophy*, 83 (3), 457–68.

Cohen, J. 2004: Minimalism about Human Rights: The Most We Can Hope For? *Journal of Political Philosophy*, 12 (2), 190–213.

Cohen, M. 1984: Moral Skepticism and International Relations. *Philosophy and Public Affairs*, 13 (4), 299–346.

Copeland, B. R. and Taylor, M. S. 2003: *Trade and the Environment: Theory and Evidence.* Princeton: Princeton University Press.

Cortright, D. and Lopez, G. A. 2002: *Smart Sanctions: Targeting Economic Statecraft.* Lanham, Md.: Rowman and Littlefield Press.

Cowen, T. 2002: *Creative Destruction: How Globalization is Changing the World's Cultures.* Princeton: Princeton University Press.

Cranston, M. 1962: *What Are Human Rights?* New York: Basic Books.

Damrosch, L. F. 1993: The Civilian Impact of Economic Sanctions. In L. F. Damrosch (ed.), *Enforcing Restraint: Collective Intervention in Internal Conflicts*, New York: Council on Foreign Relations Press, 274–315.

Damrosch, L. F. 1994: The Collective Enforcement of International Norms through Economic Sanctions. *Ethics and International Affairs*, 8, 60–80.

Dasgupta, S., Mody, A., Roy, S. and Wheeler, D. 1995: *Environmental Regulation and Development: A Cross-Country Empirical Analysis*. World Bank Policy Research Working Paper 1448. <http://econ.worldbank.org/files/807_wps1448.pdf>

DeLong, J. B. 2004: Should We Still Support Untrammelled International Capital Mobility? Or are Capital Controls Less Evil than we once Believed? *The Economists' Voice*, 1 (1), <http://www.bepress.com/ev/vol1/iss1/art1>

Denny, C. 2004: Suharto, Marcos, and Mobuto Head Corruption Table with $50bn Scams. *The Guardian*, March 26.

Diamond, J. 1997: *Guns, Germs, and Steel: The Fates of Human Societies*. New York: W. W. Norton.

Dollar, D. 2004: *Globalization, Poverty, and Inequality since 1980*. World Bank Policy Research Working Paper 3333. <http://econ.worldbank.org/files/39000_wps3333.pdf>

Dollar, D. and Kraay, A. 2002: Growth is Good for the Poor. *Journal of Economic Growth*, 7 (3), 195–225.

Dommen, C. 2002: Raising Human Rights Concerns in the World Trade Organization: Actors, Processes and Possible Strategies. *Human Rights Quarterly*, 24 (1), 1–50.

Donnelly, J. 1998: *International Human Rights*, 2nd edn. Boulder, Colo.: Westview Press.

Donnelly, J. 1999: Human Rights and Asian Values: A Defense of "Western" Universalism. In J. R. Bauer and D. A. Bell (eds), *The East Asian Challenge for Human Rights*, New York: Cambridge University Press, 60–87.

Donnelly, J. 2003: *Universal Human Rights in Theory and Practice*, 2nd edn. Ithaca, NY: Cornell University Press.

Drinan, R. F. 2001: *The Mobilization of Shame: A World View of Human Rights*. New Haven: Yale University Press.

Dunn, R. S. 1979: *The Age of Religious Wars: 1559–1715*, 2nd edn. New York: W. W. Norton.

Dworkin, R. 1977: *Taking Rights Seriously*. Cambridge, Mass.: Harvard University Press.

Dworkin, R. 1984: Rights as Trumps. In J. Waldron (ed.), *Theories of Rights*, New York: Oxford University Press, 153–67.

Easterlin, R. A. 1996: *Growth Triumphant: The Twenty-first Century in Historical Perspective*. Ann Arbor: University of Michigan Press.

Edmundson, W. 1998: Legitimate Authority without Political Obligation. *Law and Philosophy*, 17 (1), 43–60.

Egan, T. 2004: Big Farms Reap Two Harvests with Subsidies a Bumper Crop. *New York Times*, Dec. 26., sec.1, p. 36. <http://www.nytimes.com/2004/12/26/national/26farm.html>

Ehrlich, P. R. 1968: *The Population Bomb*. New York: Ballantine Books.

Emmerson, D. K. 1995: Singapore and the "Asian Values" Debate. *Journal of Democracy*, 6 (4), 95–105.

Englehart, N. A. 2000: Rights and Culture in the Asian Values Argument: The Rise and Fall of Confucian Ethics in Singapore. *Human Rights Quarterly*, 22 (2), 548–68.

Estlund, D. M. 2003: The Democracy/Contractualism Analogy. *Philosophy and Public Affairs*, 31 (4), 387–412.

Esty, D. C. 1993: GATTing the Greens: Not Just Greening the GATT. *Foreign Affairs*, 72 (5), 32–6.

Farer, T. J. 2003: Humanitarian Intervention before and after 9/11: Legality and Legitimacy. In J. L. Holzgrefe and R. O. Keohane (eds), *Humanitarian Intervention: Ethical, Legal, and Political Dimensions*, New York: Cambridge University Press, 53–89.

Freeman, M. 2002: *Human Rights: An Interdisciplinary Approach*. Cambridge: Polity.

Frei, C. 2001: *Hans J. Morgenthau: An Intellectual Biography*. Baton Rouge, La.: Louisiana State University Press.

Friedman, T. L. 1999: *The Lexus and the Olive Tree*. New York: Farrar, Straus, and Giroux.

Gardiner, S. M. 2004: Ethics and Global Climate Change. *Ethics*, 114 (3), 555–600.

Gellner, E. 1983: *Nations and Nationalism*. Ithaca, NY: Cornell University Press.

Glendon, M. A. 2001: *A World Made New: Eleanor Roosevelt and the Universal Declaration of Human Rights*. New York: Random House.

Glover, J. 1999: *Humanity: A Moral History of the Twentieth Century*. New Haven: Yale University Press.

Gomberg, P. 1990: Patriotism is like Racism. *Ethics*, 101 (1), 144–50.

Goodin, R. E. 1988: What is so Special about Our Fellow Countrymen? *Ethics*, 98 (4), 663–86.

Gourevitch, P. 1998: *We Wish to Inform you that Tomorrow we will be Killed with our Families: Stories from Rwanda*. New York: Farrar, Straus, and Giroux.

Grether, J. M. and de Melo, J. 2003: *Globalization and Dirty Industries: Do Pollution Havens Matter?* National Bureau of Economic Research Working Paper 9776. <http://papers.nber.org/papers/W9776.pdf>

Grieco, J. M. 1993a: Anarchy and the Limits of Cooperation: A Realist Critique of the Newest Liberal Institutionalism. In D. A. Baldwin (ed.), *Neorealism and Neoliberalism: The Contemporary Debate*, New York: Columbia University Press, 116–40.

Grieco, J. M. 1993b: Understanding the Problem of International Cooperation: The Limits of Neoliberal Institutionalism and the Future of Realist Theory. In D. A. Baldwin (ed.), *Neorealism and Neoliberalism: The Contemporary Debate*, New York: Columbia University Press, 301–38.

Habermas, J. 2002: On Legitimation through Human Rights. In P. D. Greiff and C. Cronin (eds), *Global Justice and Transnational Politics*, Cambridge, Mass.: MIT Press, 197–214.

Halperin, M. H., Siegle, J. T. and Weinstein, M. M. 2005: *The Democracy Advantage: How Democracies Promote Prosperity and Peace*. New York: Routledge.

Hampshire, S. 1989: *Innocence and Experience*. Cambridge, Mass.: Harvard University Press.

Hampshire, S. 2000: *Justice is Conflict*. Princeton: Princeton University Press.

Hardin, G. 1996: Lifeboat Ethics: The Case against Helping the Poor. In W. Aiken and H. LaFollette (eds), *World Hunger and Morality*, 2nd edn, Upper Saddle River, NJ: Prentice-Hall, 5–15.

Harman, G. and Thomson, J. J. 1996: *Moral Relativism and Moral Objectivity*. Malden, Mass.: Blackwell.

Hechter, M. 2000a: *Containing Nationalism*. New York: Oxford University Press.

Hechter, M. 2000b: Nationalism and Rationality. *Studies in Comparative International Development*, 35 (1), 3–19.

Hegel, G. W. F. [1821] 1991: *Elements of the Philosophy of Right*, ed. A. Wood, trans. H. B. Nisbet. New York: Cambridge University Press.

Herodotus [440 BCE] 1954: *The Histories*, trans. Aubrey de Sélincourt. New York: Penguin Books.

Hobbes, T. [1660] 1994: *Leviathan*, ed. E. Curley. Indianapolis: Hackett Publishing.

Holmes, S. and Sunstein, C. R. 1999: *The Cost of Rights: Why Liberty Depends on Taxes*. New York: W. W. Norton and Co.

Holzgrefe, J. L. 2003: The Humanitarian Intervention Debate. In J. L. Holzgrefe and R. O. Keohane (eds), *Humanitarian Intervention: Ethical, Legal, and Political Dimensions*, New York: Cambridge University Press, 15–52.

Ignatieff, M. 2001: *Human Rights as Politics and Idolatry*, ed. A. Gumann. Princeton: Princeton University Press.

Ignatieff, M. 2003: State Failure and Nation-Building. In J. L. Holzgrefe and R. O. Keohane (eds), *Humanitarian Intervention: Ethical, Legal, and Political Dimensions*, New York: Cambridge University Press, 299–321.

Interagency Council on Homelessness 1999: *Homelessness: Programs and the Peoples They Serve*. Washington, DC: United States Department of Housing and Urban Development. <http://www.huduser.org/publications/homeless/homelessness/highrpt.html>; chapter 5, "Income, Income Sources, and Employment" at <http://www.huduser.org/Publications/pdf/home_tech/tchap-05.pdf>

International Forum on Globalization 2002: *Alternatives to Economic Globalization: A Better World is Possible*. San Francisco: Berrett-Koehler Publishers.

International Labour Organization 2002: *A Future without Child Labour*. <http://www.ilo.org/dyn/declaris/declarationweb.indexpage>

Jones, C. 1999: *Global Justice: Defending Cosmopolitanism*. New York: Oxford University Press.

Jones, K. 2004: *Who's Afraid of the WTO?* New York: Oxford University Press.

Judah, T. 2002: *Kosovo: War and Revenge*, 2nd edn. New Haven: Yale University Press.

Kant, I. [1797] 1996: *The Metaphysics of Morals*, ed. and trans. M. Gregor. New York: Cambridge University Press.

Kapoor, S. 2004: The Currency Transaction Tax: Enhancing Financial Stability and Financing Development. <http://www.waronwant.org/?lid=9100&cc=1>

Kasa, K. 1999: Time for a Tobin Tax? *The Federal Reserve Bank of San Francisco Economic Letter*, 99 (12) (Apr. 9), <http://www.frbsf.org/econrsrch/wklyltr/wklyltr99/el99-12.html>

Kausikan, B. 1993: Asia's Different Standard. *Foreign Policy*, 92 (Fall), 24–41.

Kausikan, B. 1997: Governance that Works. *Journal of Democracy*, 8 (2), 24–34.

Keller, S. 2005: Patriotism as Bad Faith. *Ethics*, 115 (3), 563–92.

Kelly, E. 2004: Human Rights as Foreign Policy Imperatives. In D. K. Chatterjee (ed.), *The Ethics of Assistance: Morality and the Distant Needy*, New York: Cambridge University Press, 177–92.

Kennan, G. F. 1951: *American Diplomacy 1900–1950*. Chicago: University of Chicago Press.

Keohane, R. O. 1986: Realism, Neorealism and the Study of World Politics. In R. O. Keohane (ed.), *Neorealism and its Critics*, New York: Columbia University Press, 1–26.

Keohane, R. O. and Nye, J. S. 2001: *Power and Interdependence*, 3rd edn. New York: Longman Publishers.

Kitching, G. 2001: *Seeking Social Justice through Globalization: Escaping a Nationalist Perspective*. University Park, Pa.: Pennsylvania State University Press.

Kolers, A. 2002: The Territorial State in Cosmopolitan Justice. *Social Theory and Practice*, 28 (1), 29–50.

Krasner, S. D. 1999: *Sovereignty: Organized Hypocrisy*. Princeton: Princeton University Press.

Kremer, M. and Jayachandran, S. 2002: *Odious Debt*. National Bureau of Economic Research, Working Paper 8953. <http:/www.uber. org/papers/w8953>

Kuznets, S. 1955: Economic Growth and Income Inequality. *American Economic Review*, 45 (1), 1–28.

Kuznets, S. 1973: Modern Economic Growth: Findings and Reflections. In *Population, Capital, and Growth: Selected Essays*, New York: W. W. Norton, 165–84.

Kymlicka, W. 1989: *Liberalism, Community, and Culture*. New York: Oxford University Press.

Kymlicka, W. 1990: *Contemporary Political Philosophy: An Introduction*. Oxford: Clarendon Press.

Kymlicka, W. 1995: *Multicultural Citizenship*. New York: Oxford University Press.

Kymlicka, W. 1996: Social Unity in a Liberal State. *Social Philosophy and Policy*, 13 (1), 105–36.

Laden, A. S. 2002: Democratic Legitimacy and the 2000 Election. *Law and Philosophy*, 21 (2), 197–220.

Lango, J. W. 2001: Is Armed Humanitarian Intervention to Stop Mass Killing Morally Obligatory? *Public Affairs Quarterly*, 15 (3), 173–91.

Lee, E. 1997: Globalization and Labour Standards: A Review of Issues. *International Labour Review*, 136 (2), 173–89.

Luban, D. 2002: Intervention and Civilization: Some Unhappy Lessons of the Kosovo War. In P. D. Greiff and C. Cronin (eds), *Global Justice and Transnational Politics*, Cambridge, Mass.: MIT Press, 79–115.

Lustick, I. S., Miodownik, D. and Eidelson, R. J. 2004: Secessionism in Multicultural States: Does Sharing Power Prevent or Encourage It? *American Political Science Review*, 98 (2), 209–29.

Lyons, D. 1976: Ethical Relativism and the Problem of Incoherence. *Ethics*, 86 (3), 107–21.

MacIntyre, A. 1984: *After Virtue*, 2nd edn. Notre Dame, Ind.: University of Notre Dame Press.

Malcolm, N. 1998: *Kosovo: A Short History*. New York: New York University Press.

Mandelbaum, M. 1999: A Perfect Failure: NATO's War against Yugoslavia. *Foreign Affairs*, 79 (5), 2–8.

Mandle, J. 1999: The Reasonable in Justice as Fairness. *Canadian Journal of Philosophy*, 29 (1), 75–108.

Mandle, J. 2000a: Globalization and Justice. *Annals of the American Academy of Political and Social Science*, 570 (July), 126–39.

Mandle, J. 2000b: *What's Left of Liberalism?: An Interpretation and Defense of Justice as Fairness.* Lanham, Md.: Lexington Books.

Mandle, J. 2003: Review of Moellendorf, *Cosmopolitan Justice. Utilitas,* 15 (1), 123–6.

Mandle, J. 2005: Tolerating Injustice. In G. Brock and H. Brighouse (eds), *The Political Philosophy of Cosmopolitanism,* New York: Cambridge University Press, 219–33.

Mandle, J. forthcoming: Nielsen's Just Globalization. *Economics and Philosophy.*

Mandle, J. R. 2003: *Globalization and the Poor.* New York: Cambridge University Press.

Margalit, A. and Raz, J. 1990: National Self-Determination. *Journal of Philosophy,* 87 (9), 439–61.

Maritain, J. 1949: Introduction. In *Human Rights: Comments and Interpretations,* ed. UNESCO, New York: Columbia University Press, 9–17.

Marland, G. and Boden, T. 1996: Ranking of the World's Countries by 1996 CO_2 per capita Emission Rates. <http://cdiac.ornl.gov/trends/emis/top96.cap>

Martin, L. L. 1992: *Coercive Cooperation: Explaining Multilateral Economic Sanctions.* Princeton: Princeton University Press.

McCarthy, T. 1997: On the Idea of a Reasonable Law of Peoples. In J. Bohman and M. Lutz-Bachmann (eds), *Perpetual Peace: Essays on Kant's Cosmopolitan Ideal,* Cambridge, Mass.: MIT Press, 201–17.

McGarry, J. 1998: "Orphans of Secession": National Pluralism in Secessionist Regions and Post-Secession States. In M. Moore (ed.), *National Self-Determination and Secession,* New York: Oxford University Press, 215–32.

Mearsheimer, J. J. 2001: *The Tragedy of Great Power Politics.* New York: W. W. Norton.

Mill, J. S. [1861] 1991: *Considerations on Representative Government.* In *On Liberty and Other Essays,* ed. J. Gray, New York: Oxford University Press, 203–467.

Miller, D. 1995: *On Nationality.* Oxford: Clarendon Press.

Miller, D. 1998a: The Limits of Cosmopolitan Justice. In D. R. Mapel and T. Nardin (eds), *International Society: Diverse Ethical Perspectives,* Princeton: Princeton University Press, 164–81.

Miller, D. 1998b: Secession and the Principle of Nationality. In J. Couture, K. Nielsen, and M. Seymour (eds), *Rethinking Nationalism,* Canadian Journal of Philosophy suppl. vol. 22 (1996), Calgary, Alberta: University of Calgary Press, 261–82.

Miller, D. 1999: Justice and Global Inequality. In A. Hurrell and N. Woods (eds), *Inequality, Globalization, and World Politics,* New York: Oxford University Press, 187–210.

Miller, D. 2004: National Responsibility and International Justice. In D. K. Chatterjee (ed.), *The Ethics of Assistance: Morality and the Distant Needy*, New York: Cambridge University Press, 123–43.

Miller, J. J. 2003: J. S. Mill on Plural Voting. *History of Political Thought*, 24 (4), 647–67.

Miller, R. W. 2003: Respectable Oppressors, Hypocritical Liberators: Morality, Intervention, and Reality. In D. K. Chatterjee and D. E. Scheid (eds), *Ethics and Foreign Intervention*, New York: Cambridge University Press, 215–50.

Miller, R. W. 2004a: Beneficence, Duty, and Distance. *Philosophy and Public Affairs*, 32 (4), 357–83.

Miller, R. W. 2004b: Cosmopolitanism and its Limits: Comments on *Cosmopolitan Justice*. *Theoria*, 104 (Aug.), 38–53.

Miller, R. W. 2004c: Moral Closeness and World Community. In D. K. Chatterjee (ed.), *The Ethics of Assistance: Morality and the Distant Needy*, New York: Cambridge University Press, 101–22.

Milner, H. 1993: The Assumption of Anarchy in International Relations Theory: A Critique. In D. A. Baldwin (ed.), *Neorealism and Neoliberalism: The Contemporary Debate*, New York: Columbia University Press, 143–69.

Miščević, N. 2001: *Nationalism and Beyond: Introducing Moral Debate about Values*. New York: Central European University Press.

Mittal, A. 2002: Giving away the Farm: The 2002 Farm Bill. *Backgrounder*, 8 (3), <http://www.foodfirst.org/pubs/backgrdrs/2002/s02v8n3.html>

Moellendorf, D. 2002: *Cosmopolitan Justice*. Boulder, Colo.: Westview Press.

Moellendorf, D. 2004: *Cosmopolitan Justice* Reconsidered. *Theoria*, 104 (Aug.), 203–25.

Montaigne, M. [1580] 1987: *The Complete Essays*, ed. and trans. M. A. Screech. New York: Penguin Books.

Moody-Adams, M. M. 1997: *Fieldwork in Familiar Places: Morality, Culture, and Philosophy*. Cambridge, Mass.: Harvard University Press.

Morgenthau, H. J. 1951: *In Defense of the National Interest: A Critical Examination of American Foreign Policy*. New York: Alfred A. Knopf.

Morgenthau, H. J. and Thompson, K. W. 1985: *Politics among Nations: The Struggle for Power and Peace*, 6th edn. New York: Alfred A. Knopf.

Morsink, J. 1999: *The Universal Declaration of Human Rights: Origins, Drafting, and Intent*. Philadelphia: University of Pennsylvania Press.

Mutua, M. 2002: *Human Rights: A Political and Cultural Critique*. Philadelphia: University of Pennsylvania Press.

Nagel, T. 1986: *The View from Nowhere*. New York: Oxford University Press.

Neier, A. 2000: Economic Sanctions and Human Rights. In S. Power and G. Allison (eds), *Realizing Human Rights: Moving from Inspiration to Impact*, New York: St Martin's Press, 291–308.

Newport, F. 2004: Third of Americans Say Evidence Has Supported Darwin's Evolution Theory. *The Gallup Organization*. <http://www.gallup.com/poll/content/login.aspx?ci=14107>

Nickel, J. W. 1987: *Making Sense of Human Rights: Philosophical Reflections on the Universal Declaration of Human Rights*. Berkeley: University of California Press.

Nielsen, K. 2003: *Globalization and Justice*. Amherst, NY: Humanity Books.

Nietzsche, F. [1887] 1998: *On the Genealogy of Morality: A Polemic*, ed. and trans. M. Clark and A. J. Swensen. Indianapolis: Hackett Publishing.

Nussbaum, M. C. 1996: *For Love of Country: Debating the Limits of Patriotism*, ed. J. Cohen. Boston: Beacon Press.

Nussbaum, M. C. 2004: Women and Theories of Global Justice: Our Need for New Paradigms. In D. K. Chatterjee (ed.), *The Ethics of Assistance: Morality and the Distant Needy*, New York: Cambridge University Press, 147–76.

Organization for Economic Cooperation and Development 1996: *Trade, Employment and Labour Standards: A Study of Core Workers' Rights and International Trade*. Paris: OECD.

Organization for Economic Cooperation and Development 2004: Net Official Development Assistance in 2003. <http://www.oecd.org/dataoecd/42/61/31504039.pdf>

Oxfam 2002a: *Europe's Double Standards: How the EU Should Reform its Trade Policies with the Developing World*. <http://www.oxfam.org/eng/pdfs/pp0204_Europes_Double_Standards.pdf>

Oxfam 2002b: *Rigged Rules and Double Standards: Trade, Globalization, and the Fight against Poverty*. <http://www.maketradefair.com/assets/english/report_english.pdf>

Paul VI 1967: Declaration on Religious Freedom: *Dignitatis Humanae*. <http://www.cin.org/v2relfre.html>

Payne, R. 1973: *Massacre*. New York: Macmillan.

Philpott, D. 1998: Self-Determination in Practice. In M. Moore (ed.), *National Self-Determination and Secession*, New York: Oxford University Press, 79–102.

Pierce, A. 1996: Just War Principles and Economic Sanctions. *Ethics and International Affairs*, 10, 99–113.

Pogge, T. W. 1994: An Egalitarian Law of Peoples. *Philosophy and Public Affairs*, 23 (3), 195–224.

Pogge, T. W. 1998: A Global Resource Dividend. In D. A. Crocker and T. Linden (eds), *The Ethics of Consumption: The Good Life, Justice, and Global Stewardship*. Lanham, Md.: Rowman and Littlefield, 501–36.

Pogge, T. W. 2001: Priorities of Global Justice. *Metaphilosophy*, 32 (1/2), 6–24.

Pogge, T. W. 2002: *World Poverty and Human Rights*. Cambridge: Polity.

Pogge, T. W. 2004a: "Assisting" the Global Poor. In D. K. Chatterjee (ed.), *The Ethics of Assistance: Morality and the Distant Needy*, New York: Cambridge University Press, 260–88.

Pogge, T. W. 2004b: The First United Nations Millennium Development Goal: A Cause for Celebration? *Journal of Human Development*, 5 (3), 377–97.

Pollis, A. and Schwab, P. 1979: Human Rights: A Western Construct with Limited Applicability. In A. Pollis and P. Schwab (eds), *Human Rights: Cultural and Ideological Perspectives*, New York: Praeger Publishers, 1–18.

Powell, C. L. with Persico, J. 1996: *My American Journey*, paperback edn. New York: Ballantine Press.

Power, S. 2002: *"A Problem from Hell": America and the Age of Genocide*. New York: Basic Books.

Przeworski, A. and Limongi, F. 1993: Political Regimes and Economic Growth. *Journal of Economic Perspectives*, 7 (3), 51–69.

Quiggin, J. 2001: Globalization and Economic Sovereignty. *Journal of Political Philosophy*, 9 (1), 56–80.

Rawls, J. 1996: *Political Liberalism*, expanded paperback edn. New York: Columbia University Press.

Rawls, J. 1999a: *A Theory of Justice*, rev. edn. Cambridge, Mass.: Harvard University Press.

Rawls, J. 1999b: *The Law of Peoples with "The Idea of Public Reason Revisited"*. Cambridge, Mass.: Harvard University Press.

Rawls, J. 2001: *Justice as Fairness: A Restatement*, ed. E. Kelly. Cambridge, Mass.: Harvard University Press.

Reddy, S. G. and Pogge, T. W. 2003: How *Not* to Count the Poor. <http://www.columbia.edu/~sr793/count.pdf>

Risse, T. and Sikkink, K. 1999: The Socialization of International Human Rights Norms into Domestic Practices: Introduction. In T. Risse, S. C. Ropp and K. Sikkink (eds), *The Power of Human Rights: International Norms and Domestic Change*, New York: Cambridge University Press, 1–38.

Rorty, R. 1996: Who Are We? Moral Universalism and Economic Triage. *Diogenes*, 44 (1), 5–15.

Rorty, R. 1998: Human Rights, Rationality, and Sentimentality. In *Truth and Progress: Philosophical Papers*, vol. 3, New York: Cambridge University Press, 167–85.

Roth, K. 2004: War in Iraq: Not a Humanitarian Intervention. In *Human Rights Watch World Report 2004: Human Rights and Armed Conflict*, New York: Human Rights Watch, 13–35. <http://www.hrw.org/wr2k4/download/wr2k4.pdf>

Rummel, R. J. 1994: *Death by Government*. New Brunswick, NJ: Transaction Publishers.

Runge, C. F. 2001: A Global Environment Organization (GEO) and the World Trading System. *Journal of World Trade*, 35 (4), 399–426.

Sandel, M. J. 1998: *Liberalism and the Limits of Justice*, 2nd edn. New York: Cambridge University Press.

Scanlon, T. M. 2003: Human Rights as a Neutral Concern. In *The Difficulty of Tolerance: Essays in Political Philosophy*, New York: Cambridge University Press, 113–23.

Sen, A. 1981: *Poverty and Famines: An Essay on Entitlement and Deprivation*. New York: Oxford University Press.

Sen, A. 1994: Population: Delusion and Reality. *New York Review of Books*, 41 (15) (Sept. 22), 62–71.

Sen, A. 1997: *Human Rights and Asian Values*. New York: Carnegie Council on Ethics and International Affairs. <http://www.carnegie council.org/media/254_sen.pdf>

Sen, A. 1999: *Development as Freedom*. New York: Alfred A. Knopf.

Shue, H. 1996: *Basic Rights: Subsistence, Affluence, and U.S. Foreign Policy*, 2nd edn. Princeton: Princeton University Press.

Shue, H. 1998: Let Whatever Is Smouldering Erupt? Conditional Sovereignty, Reviewable Intervention and Rwanda 1994. In A. J. Paolini, A. P. Jarvis and C. Reus-Smit (eds), *Between Sovereignty and Global Governance: The United Nations, the State and Civil Society*, New York: St Martin's Press, 60–84.

Silberbauer, G. 1991: Ethics in Small-Scale Societies. In P. Singer (ed.), *A Companion to Ethics*, Cambridge, Mass.: Basil Blackwell, 14–28.

Singer, P. 1972: Famine, Affluence, and Morality. *Philosophy and Public Affairs*, 1 (3), 229–43.

Singer, P. 2002: *One World: The Ethics of Globalization*. New Haven: Yale University Press.

Smith, M. J. 1986: *Realist Thought from Weber to Kissinger*. Baton Rouge, La.: Louisiana State University Press.

Solana, J. 1999: NATO's Success in Kosovo. *Foreign Affairs*, 78 (6), 114–20.

Steel, R. 2004: George Kennan at 100. *New York Review of Books*, 51 (7) (Apr. 29), 8–9.

Stiglitz, J. E. 2003: *Globalization and its Discontents*, paperback edn. New York: W. W. Norton.

Sumner, W. G. 2001: Folkways. In P. Moser and T. Carson (eds), *Moral Relativism: A Reader*, New York: Oxford University Press, 69–79.

Tamir, Y. 1993: *Liberal Nationalism*. Princeton: Princeton University Press.

Tan, K. C. 2000: *Toleration, Diversity, and Global Justice*. University Park, Pa.: Pennsylvania State University Press.

Tesón, F. R. 1988: *Humanitarian Intervention: An Inquiry into Law and Morality*. Dobbs Ferry, NY: Transnational Publishers.

Thomas, D. C. 1999: The Helsinki Accords and Political Change in Eastern Europe. In T. Risse, S. C. Ropp, and K. Sikkink (eds), *The Power of Human Rights: International Norms and Domestic Change*, New York: Cambridge University Press, 205–33.

Thomas, D. C. 2001: *The Helsinki Effect: International Norms, Human Rights, and the Demise of Communism*. Princeton: Princeton University Press.

Thompson, D. F. 1976: *John Stuart Mill and Representative Government*. Princeton: Princeton University Press.

Thucydides 1998: *The Peloponnesian War*, trans. S. Lattimore. Indianapolis: Hackett Publishing Co.

Tobin, J. 1996: Prologue. In M. ul Haq, I. Kaul and I. Grunberg (eds), *The Tobin Tax: Coping with Financial Volatility*, New York: Oxford University Press, pp. ix–xviii.

Tobin, J. 1998: Financial Globalization: Can National Currencies Survive? Keynote Address to the Annual World Bank Conference on Development Economics, 1998. <http://www.worldbank.org/html/rad/abcde/tobin.pdf>

Tomasi, J. 1995: Kymlicka, Liberalism, and Respect for Cultural Minorities. *Ethics*, 105 (3), 580–603.

Ullman, R. 1999: The US and the World: An Interview with George Kennan. *New York Review of Books*, 46 (13) (Aug. 12), 4–6.

Unger, P. 1996: *Living High and Letting Die: Our Illusion of Innocence*. New York: Oxford University Press.

United Nations 1945: *Charter of the United Nations*. <http://www.un.org/aboutun/charter/>

United Nations 1948a: *Convention on the Prevention and Punishment of the Crime of Genocide*. <http://www.unhchr.ch/html/menu3/b/p_genoci.htm>

United Nations 1948b: *Universal Declaration of Human Rights*. <http://www.un.org/Overview/rights.html>

United Nations 1970: *Declaration on Principles of International Law concerning Friendly Relations and Co-operation among States in accordance with the Charter of the United Nations*. <http://www.un.org/documents/ga/res/25/ares25.htm>

United Nations 1993: *Vienna Declaration and Programme of Action*. <http://www.unhchr.ch/html/menu5/wchr.htm>

United Nations Development Programme 1998: *Human Development Report 1998*. New York: Oxford University Press. <http://hdr.undp.org/reports/global/1998/en/>

United Nations Development Programme 2003: *Human Development Report 2003: Millennium Development Goals: A Compact among Nations to End Human Poverty*. New York: Oxford University Press. <http://hdr.undp.org/reports/global/2003/>

United States Census Bureau 2004: Poverty Thresholds. <http://www.census.gov/hhes/poverty/threshld.html>

United States Department of Commerce 1952: *Statistical Abstract of the United States 1952*. <http://www2.census.gov/prod2/statcomp/documents/1952-05.pdf>

Waldron, J. (ed.) 1987: *Nonsense upon Stilts: Bentham, Burke and Marx on the Rights of Man*. New York: Methuen.

Waldron, J. 1992: Minority Cultures and the Cosmopolitan Alternative. *University of Michigan Journal of Law Reform*, 25 (3 & 4), 751–93.

Waldron, J. 1993: Special Ties and Natural Duties. *Philosophy and Public Affairs*, 22 (1), 3–30.

Waltz, K. N. 1979: *Theory of International Politics*. New York: McGraw-Hill Publishers.

Walzer, M. 1992: The New Tribalism: Notes on a Difficult Problem. *Dissent* (Spring), 164–71.

Walzer, M. 2000: *Just and Unjust Wars: A Moral Argument with Historical Illustrations*, 3rd edn. New York: Basic Books.

Walzer, M. 2004: *Arguing about War*. New Haven: Yale University Press.

Weber, M. [1922] 1946: Structures of Power. In H. H. Gerth and C. W. Mills (trans. and ed.), *From Max Weber: Essays in Sociology*, New York: Oxford University Press, 159–79.

Weinstock, D. 2001: Constitutionalizing the Right to Secede. *Journal of Political Philosophy*, 9 (2), 182–203.

Weiss, L. 1998: *The Myth of the Powerless State*. Ithaca, NY: Cornell University Press.

Wenar, L. 2002: The Legitimacy of Peoples. In P. D. Greiff and C. Cronin (eds), *Global Justice and Transnational Politics*, Cambridge, Mass.: MIT Press, 53–76.

Wheeler, D. 2002: *Racing to the Bottom? Foreign Investment and Air Pollution in Developing Countries*. World Bank Policy Research Working Paper 2524. <http://econ.worldbank.org/files/1340_wps 2524.pdf>

Wong, D. 1984: *Moral Relativity*. Berkeley: University of California Press.

Wong, D. 1991: Relativism. In P. Singer (ed.), *A Companion to Ethics*, Cambridge, Mass.: Basil Blackwell, 442–50.

Woods, N. 2001: Making the IMF and the World Bank More Accountable. *International Affairs*, 77 (1), 83–100.

World Bank Data Query, <http://devdata.worldbank.org/data-query>.

World Bank 2001: *World Development Report 2000/2001: Attacking Poverty*. Overview: <http://siteresources.worldbank.org/INT POVERTY/Resources/WDR/overview.pdf>

World Conference on Human Rights 1993: *Final Declaration of the Regional Meeting for Asia of the World Conference on Human Rights* ["Bangkok Declaration"]. <http://law.hku.hk/lawgovtsociety/ Bangkok%20Declaration.htm>

World Health Organization 2000: *Global Water Supply and Sanitation Assessment 2000*. <http://www.who.int/docstore/water_sanitation_ health/Globassessment/Global1.htm>

World Intellectual Property Organization. <http://www.wipo.int>

Young, I. M. 1990: *Justice and the Politics of Difference*. Princeton: Princeton University Press.

Zakaria, F. 1994: Culture is Destiny: A Conversation with Lee Kuan Yew. *Foreign Affairs*, 73 (2), 109–26.

Index

agricultural subsidies 132–4, 143, 158 n.2
Albright, M. 97
Anderson, B. 38–9
An-Na'Im, A. 51
Aristotle 81, 152 n.3
Asian financial crisis 104, 110, 135
"Asian values" challenge to human rights 63–71, 76

bananas 142–3
Bangladesh *see* East Pakistan
Barber, B. 145
Baron, H. 90
basic structure of society 20–1, 23, 25–7, 95, 99, 107–8, 110, 112
see also justice, concept of; justice, domestic principles of
Beitz, C. 1, 80, 102
Bell, D. 69–70
Benedict, R. 9
benign neglect (of culture) 147–8
Bentham, J. 19, 93, 95
Bhagwati, J. 125, 134, 137, 140, 142–3
Blake, M. 112–3, 157 n.8
Bretton Woods monetary system 126–7, 136

Buchanan, A. 39, 43, 47, 50, 52, 56, 62–3, 68, 89–92, 155–6 n.7, 155–6 n.7
see also justice, natural duty of; secession

Calhoun, C. 36–7
Catholic Church 22–3
see also religion
Chomsky, N. 4
Christie, K. 70
Coady, C. 94, 95
colonialism 16, 74, 95, 100, 102, 157 n.9
comprehensive doctrines 17–8, 20, 22–7, 42–3, 44, 50–1, 53, 64, 86, 88, 107, 149
see also justice, political conception of; religion
Convention on Genocide 73–4, 100
cosmopolitanism 35, 41–3, 88, 106–13, 122, 148
Cowen, T. 145–6
Cranston, M. 60–2, 154 n.1
culture 37–9, 53, 65, 88, 117–8, 145–9, 151, 159 n.7

debt bondage 138
decent hierarchical societies 78–81, 85–6, 117, 150, 155 n.2, 156 n.8

democracy 26, 30, 54, 59, 66–7, 70, 78, 84–5, 94, 116
development, economic 65–7, 104–5, 117–21, 134–6, 138, 146
see also trade liberalization
Diamond, J. 12
Dollar, D. 104
Donnelly, J. 51, 64, 67, 69, 77
Drinan, R. 73
Dulles, J. 74
dumping *see* agricultural subsidies
duties, negative and positive 48–50, 62–3, 107, 114–17, 122
see also justice, natural duty of
Dworkin, R. 45–6

East Pakistan 106, 157 n.4
Easterlin, R. 120
Emmerson, D. 70
environment 113, 121–2, 124, 137–42, 144, 148–9, 159 n.6
see also Global Environmental Organization (GEO); Global Resource Dividend (GRD)

fair equality of opportunity 25–6, 108–10
see also justice, domestic principles of
Farer, T. 93, 97–8
financial liberalization 134–7, 158–9 n.3
see also trade liberalization; Tobin Tax
foreign direct assistance 122–3, 132–3
free trade *see* trade liberalization
Freeman, M. 53, 69–70, 73
Friedman, T. 145

General Agreement on Tariffs and Trade (GATT) 127–9, 135, 137, 139
see also World Trade Organization
Glendon, M. 72–6
Global Environmental Organization (GEO) 144
Global Resource Dividend (GRD) 121–3, 135, 137, 144

Goodin, R. 40, 42
Gourevitch, P. 100

Habermas, J. 82–3
Halperin, M., et. al. 66, 116
Hampshire, S. 18, 52
Hardin, G. 61, 119–20
Hegel, G. 5, 84
Helsinki Final Act 77
Herodotus 8–11
Hippocratic principle 4
Hobbes, T. 19, 32–4, 81, 87
human rights, list of 52
humanitarian intervention 92–101

Ignatieff, M. 46, 52, 89, 91, 94–5
inequality 38–40, 56, 78, 105–6, 111–13, 118–9
see also fair equality of opportunity; justice, domestic principles of
International Bank for Reconstruction and Development *see* World Bank
international borrowing privilege 115–16, 118
see also odious debt
International Forum on Globalization 130–1, 145
International Labor Organization (ILO) 138, 141–2, 144
International Monetary Fund (IMF) 116, 126, 135, 143–4
international resource privilege 115–16, 118

Jones, C. 42
Jones, K. 127–8, 133–4, 137, 139, 144
just cause *see* humanitarian intervention
justice, concept of 17–20, 25–6
see also basic structure of society; liberalism; justice, natural duty of
justice, domestic principles of 25–6, 55–56, 78–9, 107–9, 117, 138, 148, 159 n.7
see also cosmopolitanism; fair equality of opportunity; inequality; nationalism; realism

justice, natural duty of 47, 83, 102,
   117, 148
   see also duties, negative and
   positive
justice, political conception of 15,
   19–27, 44, 80, 86, 107, 112, 152
   n.1, 152 n.2, 154 n.2, 157 n.5
   see also basic structure of society;
   comprehensive doctrines;
   liberalism; religion

Kant, I. 81, 83–4
Kausikan, B. 65, 67–70
Kelly, E. 100–1
Kennan, G. 30, 35, 154 n.2
Keohane, R. 28–9, 32
Kitching, G. 119, 125–7, 131, 142
Kosovo 3–6
Krasner, S. 16, 72
Kuznets, S. 118
Kymlicka, W. 9–10, 56, 147, 156
   n.10

labor standards 137–42, 148–9
   see also International Labor
   Organization
last resort *see* humanitarian
   intervention
law 21, 23, 32–34, 36, 46, 49, 52–4,
   60–1, 81–8, 91, 117, 139
   see also basic structure of society;
   state
Lee Kuan Yew 65–8
liberalism 15–27, 55–6, 78–80, 86,
   112, 150
   see also comprehensive doctrine;
   justice, domestic principles of;
   justice, political conception of;
   religion
Luban, D. 3, 99–100

MacIntyre, A. 59–60
Mandle, J. R. 128, 142–3
Maori 12–4
Margalit, A. 37–8
Marshall Plan 122, 126, 158 n.15
McCarthy, T. 80
Mearsheimer, J. 32–4, 153 n.2
Melian dialogue 29

Mill, J. 37–8, 84, 156 n.11
Miller, D. 36, 38, 41, 43, 89, 108,
   111–12, 153 n.4
Miller, R. 96–7, 107
Mobutu Sésé-Seko 115–16
Moellendorf, D. 32, 42, 94–9,
   108–12, 156 n.12
   see also cosmopolitanism; fair
   equality of opportunity;
   humanitarian intervention
Montaigne, M. 9
Moody-Adams, M. 11, 13
"moralizer" 7–8, 14, 34–5, 151
Morgenthau, H. 30–5, 153 n.2
Moriori 12–3
Morsink, J. 72, 74–5
mortality revolution 120–1
Myanmar (Burma) 70

Nagel, T. 10
nation 36–9, 42
   see also nationalism; state
nationalism 35–43, 71, 88–90, 111,
   122,
NATO 2–7
Nickel, J. 57
Nielsen, K. 129, 150
Nietzsche, F. 81–2
non-governmental organizations
   (NGOs) 2, 68–70, 75, 77
North American Free Trade
   Agreement (NAFTA) 139
Nussbaum, M. 40, 64

odious debt 115–16
outlaw state 79
   see also decent hierarchical society
Oxfam 131–3, 144, 159 n.5

Peace of Westphalia 16
   see also Westphalian sovereignty
Peloponnesian War 29
philosophy 1–8, 15, 17, 106, 149
Pogge, T. 36, 46–8, 103–6, 109,
   114–18, 121–4, 130, 132, 135,
   156 n.1, 157–8 n.10, 158 n.11
   see also global resource dividend;
   international borrowing privilege;
   international resource privilege

political liberalism *see* justice, political conception of
Powell, C. 97
proper authorization *see* humanitarian intervention; United Nations Security Council
proportionality *see* humanitarian intervention

"race to the bottom" 140–2
 see also environment; labor standards
Rawls, J. 1–3, 6, 15–6, 20, 47, 51, 78–86, 95, 107–8, 113, 117–18, 147, 149–51, 154 n.2, 154 n.3, 155 n.2, 156 n.8, 158 n.11, 158 n.13
 see also decent hierarchical society; liberalism; justice, political conception of; realistic utopia
Raz, J. 37–8
realism 1, 4, 28–35, 42, 71, 87
realistic utopia 5–6, 149–51
Reddy, S. 156 n.1
relativism 7–15
religion 15–27, 37, 39, 42, 44, 51–3, 55–6, 64, 68, 74, 78, 86, 95, 100,
Roosevelt, E. 73–4
Rorty, R. 6–7, 105
Roth, K. 98
Rwanda 92, 100–1

Sandel, M. 17–8
secession 89–92, 155–6 n.7
 see also nation; nationalism; state
Sen, A. 64–7, 120–1
Shue, H. 1, 46, 53–5, 57–8, 61–2, 96, 99
Silberbauer, G. 11
Singapore 70, 92
 see also "Asian Values" challenge to human rights; Lee Kwan Yew; Kausikan, B.
Singer, P. 106–7, 121, 139
slavery 3, 6, 10, 64, 138
 see also debt bondage
state 16–7, 36, 38–9, 43, 72, 81–2, 87–93, 112–13, 142

see also basic structure of society; law; nation; nationalism; secession; Westphalian sovereignty
steel 144
Stiglitz, J. 133, 135–6, 143

Tamir, Y. 41
Tan, K. 80, 113
terrorism 124
Tesón, F. 94
Thirty Years' War 16
Thomas, D. 77
Thomson, J. 10
Thucydides 29, 153 n.1
Tobin, J. 136–7
 see also financial liberalization; Tobin Tax
Tobin Tax 136–7, 144
trade liberalization 110–13, 125–35, 139–43, 150
 see also agricultural subsidies; financial liberalization; General Agreement on Tariffs and Trade; NAFTA; World Trade Organization
Trade-Related Intellectual Property (TRIPs) 137
Trade-Related Investment Measures (TRIMs) 135, 137
tuna 139–40

United Nations, Charter of 72–3, 76, 154 n.4
 see also Universal Declaration of Human Rights; Vienna Conference on Human Rights
United Nations Educational, Scientific and Cultural Organization (UNESCO) 51, 73–4
United Nations Security Council 2, 4, 95–6, 100
 see also humanitarian intervention
Universal Declaration of Human Rights (UDHR) 44, 51, 57, 60, 63, 71–7, 103–4
"universalist" 8
 see also "moralizer", relativism

Vienna Conference on Human Rights 76

Waldron, J. 86, 147
"walling off" 10
Walzer, M. 89, 94–5, 98–9, 156 n.11
Washington, G. 10
Weinstock, M. 90
Westphalian sovereignty 16, 72–3,
    93
    see also state
Wong, D. 8–9, 13–4

World Bank 126, 133, 135, 143–4,
    158 n.15
World Trade Organization (WTO)
    128–9, 132–4, 137, 139–40,
    142–4, 157 n.9

Young, I. 84–5

Zaire 115–16